Edward P. Crowell, Essex, Mass. First Congregational Church, F. H Palmer

Two Centuries of Church History

celebration of the two hundredth anniversary of the organization of the

Congregational church & parish in Essex, Mass., August 19-22, 1883

Edward P. Crowell, Essex, Mass. First Congregational Church, F. H Palmer

Two Centuries of Church History
celebration of the two hundredth anniversary of the organization of the Congregational church & parish in Essex, Mass., August 19-22, 1883

ISBN/EAN: 9783337237448

Printed in Europe, USA, Canada, Australia, Japan

Cover: Foto ©ninafisch / pixelio.de

More available books at **www.hansebooks.com**

Two Centuries of Church History

CELEBRATION

OF THE

TWO HUNDREDTH ANNIVERSARY

OF THE ORGANIZATION

OF THE

Congregational Church & Parish

IN

ESSEX, MASS.,

AUGUST 19-22, 1883.

PRELIMINARY.

At a meeting of the Congregational Church in Essex held January 9th, 1883, it was voted—"That this Church observe the two hundredth anniversary of its organization by holding services appropriate to the occasion."

At a subsequent meeting it was voted that the anniversary have reference to the organization of the Parish as well as of the Church and the parish were invited to join in the proposed celebration.

A committee of the church was appointed and at the Annual Parish meeting, held April 16th, a committee was chosen to unite with the committee of the church in making all necessary arrangements for the occasion.

The following are the committees:

Committee of the Church.

Dea. Caleb S. Gage,   Rufus Choate,   Reuben Morris,
And the Acting Pastor, Ex Officio.

Committee of the Parish.

Addison Cogswell,   Dea. Caleb Cogswell,
Henry W. Mears.

On Entertainment.

Frank E. Burnham,   Mrs. Hervey Burnham,
Henry W. Mears,   Mrs. Mary C. Osgood,
Reuben Morris,   Mrs. D. Webster Cogswell,
Joseph Procter, Jr.,   Mrs. Philip T. Adams,
D. Brainard Burnham,   Mrs. Josiah Low,
Francis Haskell,   Miss Lizzie M. Norton.

On Finance.
D. BRAINARD BURNHAM.   JOSEPH PROCTER, JR.

On Decorations.
MISS ELLEN BOYD.   MRS. ALBERT L. BUTLER.
MRS. GEORGE PROCTER.   MRS. GEORGE A. FULLER.
RUFUS CHOATE.

On Music.
WILLIAM C. CHOATE.   RUFUS CHOATE.
MRS. HERVEY BURNHAM.   MISS CARRIE O. SPOFFORD.

On the Tent.
HENRY W. MEARS.

On Printing.
REV. F. H. PALMER.   RUFUS CHOATE.

ORDER OF EXERCISES.

Sunday, August 19th, at 2 p.m.

MEMORIAL SERMON   by Rev. F. H. Palmer, Acting Pastor.

Wednesday, August 22nd, 9.30 a.m.

VOLUNTARY.

ANTHEM . . . "Strike the Cymbal."
INVOCATION . . by Rev. F. H. Palmer, Acting Pastor.
READING OF SCRIPTURE . by Ex Pastor Rev. J. L. Harris.
PRAYER . . by Ex Pastor Rev. D. A. Morehouse.
ADDRESS OF WELCOME by the Acting Pastor.
HISTORICAL DISCOURSE
                by Rev. Prof. E. P. Crowell of Amherst College.
HYMN (Old Style) . . . Lined off by Bro. Rufus Choate.
ADDRESS ON REV. JOHN WISE
                by Rev. H. M. Dexter, D.D., of Boston.

HYMN.

At the close of the morning services the congregation adjourned to the neighboring cemetery where prayer was offered at the grave of Rev. John Wise by Prof. E. A. Park, D.D., of Andover, Mass.

1–2.30 p.m.
COLLATION, IN THE VESTRY.
2.30 p.m.

ANTHEM . . . . "Denmark."
GREETING FROM THE MOTHER CHURCH,
            by Rev. E. B. Palmer of Ipswich.
GREETING FROM SISTER CHURCHES,
            by Rev. F. G. Clark, of Gloucester.
REMINISCENCES OF DR. CROWELL
            by Rev. Jeremiah Taylor, D.D., of Providence, R.I.
LETTERS.
REMARKS . . by Prof. Park of Andover.
HYMN.
BENEDICTION.
SOCIAL REUNION IN THE VESTRY 7.30 p.m.

Invitations were sent out to neighboring churches and pastors, and to all old friends and members of the church so far as their addresses could be learned. A mammoth tent was erected on the grounds of Mr. Daniel W. Low, and the weather proving auspicious, about a thousand persons assembled to listen to the public exercises. The old pulpit used in the latter part of the eighteenth century by Rev. John Cleaveland, and afterwards during the ministry of Revs. Josiah Webster, Thomas Holt, and Dr. Crowell was placed upon the platform for the accommodation of the speakers.

Rev. Mr. Palmer, Acting Pastor, presided and in his address of welcome extended a cordial greeting to all, indulged in the thoughts which the lapse of two hundred years would naturally suggest and concluded by saying that we glory in these old names which cluster around our early history as we rehearse their deeds.

At the close of the forenoon services an aged man who well remembered the raising of the present meeting house, in 1792, was introduced to the congregation. This was Mr. Andrew Burnham in his 90th year. He came forward and occupied the platform during the singing of the last hymn.

The collation which was served by the ladies at noon was one of the most bountiful ever known in the history of the town.

The music of the day, which was most excellent, was under the direction of the organist of the church Mr. William C. Choate.

The vestry and audience room were well filled during the evening where a season of social intercourse was greatly enjoyed. Brief but eloquent addresses were made by the President of the day Rev. Mr. Palmer, Ex Pastor Rev. J. L. Harris, Rev. George L. Gleason of Byfield, John Howard Burnham, Esq., of Bloomington, Ill., and Rev. D. O. Mears, D. D. of Worcester. An original Poem written for the occasion by Mrs. Elizabeth Lane of Boston, formerly a member of this society, was read by Miss Ida P. Howes.

The choir and band discoursed sweet music between the addresses. The services of the day closed with prayer by the acting pastor and the singing of the doxology.

The following account of the church decorations is taken from the *Boston Journal* of the next day:

The church interior was handsomely decorated for the occasion, apparently at much labor and expense. A large floral arch was over the altar, and in the centre were the words:

"PROFANE NOT THE COVENANT OF OUR FATHERS."

This was flanked by the dates 1683 and 1883. Suspended from the arch was a tablet inclosed in evergreen and scarlet geraniums, bearing the words of Acts x, 33, which formed the text when the present church was dedicated in 1793. A floral work suspended from the ceiling was attractive from its composition of ferns and myrtle leaves. The pulpit was almost hidden from view by gladioli and other flowers. The walls were decorated at appropriate points with ornamental crosses, wreaths and flowers in various designs. The balcony front centre was arrayed in festoons of white trimmed with trailing ivy, and the right and left of the balcony were festooned with the American colors. The balcony rail was surmounted with pots of rare exotics, and also golden rod, ferns, oak leaves, etc. There was much to please the eye in the general adornment.

The location of the first church building, raised in April 1679, was marked by flags; also that of the second house of worship raised in 1718. Some of the foundation stones of this building still remain beneath the soil. A flag waving from each corner clearly revealed the exact location of the building to many interested visitors.

The spot on which Rev. John Wise lived during the first twenty years of his ministry, was also indicated by a flag.

A wreath of evergreen upon the tombstones of Revs. Theophilus Pickering and John Cleaveland, in the old cemetery, marked the last resting place of those divines.

The tablet of slate in the monument over Mr. Wise's grave having been injured, was replaced by one of more durable quality bearing, however, the same epitaph. This gift was through the generosity of a parishioner Mr. Addison Cogswell.

Among the large company from abroad who manifested a hearty interest in the occasion were many members of the families of former pastors of the Church. The families of Pickering, Cleaveland, Crowell, Bacon, Morehouse and Harris were well represented.

The warm interest and sympathy of absent members who had returned to their former spiritual home, the devotion of the entire Parish to the duties of the hour, the presence and congratulations of many families of the town, not now in church relations with us, but whose ancestors for many generations worshipped at this altar, the delightful memories revived by the various exercises, all combined to make this a most interesting and long to be remembered Anniversary.

Memorial Sermon

BY REV. F. H. PALMER, ACTING PASTOR.

Preached on Sunday, August 19, 1883, in the First Congregational Church.*

"*For* enquire, I pray thee, *of the former age, and prepare thyself to the search of their* fathers." Job 8: 8.

On the first day of January, 1815, a sermon was preached from these words by the Rev. Robert Crowell, who had been ordained pastor of this church five months before. In the printed copies of that sermon there is an explanatory note, stating that "the following discourse consists of a compilation of facts the knowledge of which it was thought might be useful to the rising generation of this parish;" and expressing the hope "that it may serve to increase the knowledge of their fathers, and lead them, through divine grace, to imitate their pious and devout examples."

---

*In conducting the services Mr. Palmer used what is probably the oldest Bible to be found in any family in this section. It is the property of Mrs. Winthrop Low. Upon the fly-leaf it is written:

"The title page and several leaves at the beginning are missing. This Bible was without doubt brought from England by the first settlers, bearing the name of Low."

"The Old and New Testament, printed by Christopher Barker, in the year 1759." See fac simile.)

"The Whole Book of Psalms, by Sternhold, Hopkins and others, printed as follows: 'At London, printed by John Days, dwelling over Aldersgate, An. 1578. Cum Privilegio Regiae Majestatis.'"

"Susanna Low, her Book, 1667. May 19. Thomas Low, his Book. Both names appear to have been written very nearly at the same time.)

"The names of Samuel Low and John Low, written probably near 200 years ago, also are found on the blank leaves."

In the providence of God we are again reminded, by the occurrence of our two hundredth anniversary, of the appropriateness and profit of turning our glances backward and observing the events of the past, in which the successes and the failures of our forefathers have been wrought out. It is necessary to pause occasionally, at appropriate periods, and review the past. The events which make up our human experience succeed each other so rapidly,—so swift is the current that is sweeping us onward through our brief span of life toward eternity,—that we hardly realize the meaning of what is taking place around us. No age can truly estimate its own power and significance. It is the part of the future to rate the time that now is. Hence the propriety of these anniversary seasons. We are to view the past as a written page of instruction, which will teach us the meaning of God's providence, and disclose to us the value of life, and lead us to appreciate the blessings and opportunities which accrue to us from the devout and self-denying labors of those who have gone before.

More than sixty-eight years have passed away since Dr. Crowell used these words of Job's friend to turn our fathers' thoughts back to the earlier history of their *then* ancient church. That which was new in that day has become old now, and that which was old then has become very, very, old. "The fathers" upon whose "pious and devout examples" our fathers reflected, have become great-great-grandfathers to those living at the present day. We have the pious examples of many generations to reflect upon. We have the accumulated experiences of a long line of godly ancestors. We can study their deeds and their principles; and profiting by the dispassionate verdict of time upon their various doings we can judge, with some degree of accuracy, of the wisdom and earnestnesss of their lives, and of the quality of the institutions which they founded for the promotion of human happiness and for the glory of God. We can judge, too, of the progress of ideas, and of the advance that this world has been making in attainments, physical, intellectual and spiritual, since their day. We may thus find abundant cause for congratulation; we may thus learn many needed lessons, and gain many valuable encouragements which will aid us in maintaining the institutions which they have founded, and help us to hand these down, in turn, to posterity, with new demonstrations of their usefulness and power. If our present significant anniversary shall do this for us,—if our rich past shall thus instruct us, it will not be in vain that we "enquire," to-day, "of the former age," and prepare ourselves "to the search of their fathers."

It is not my purpose to review, on this occasion, the *facts* in our history in the order of their occurrence. The story of the founding of this church and the detailed history of its twelve pastorates is an interesting narrative. The fullness and accuracy with which it can and will be related, is due almost wholly to the disinterested labors of that revered pastor to whom I have already referred. And it is an especially felicitous circumstance that we may have for our historian on this occasion, one who by nature and inheritance, is so especially qualified for the task.

Without trespassing at all on the province of others who are to review the events of these two centuries of church and parish life in this community, I wish to direct your attention, to-day, to some more general matters which have a direct bearing upon the results of these fruitful years. The first and proper business of the historian is to narrate facts, to set forth events in the order of their occurrence. This is the work that is to be done for us by others. But facts and events are effects; and every effect has and must have an efficient cause behind it. It is the part of the *philosopher* to trace the events of history to their causes, and to show how and why things have happened as they have. As all philosophy is but a search for causes, and as all causes ultimately proceed from, or are merged into the one great *first cause*, which is God himself, so the philosopher in the highest exercise of his function becomes the theologian, as he traces whatever is, and has been, to the overruling providence of God. Without arrogating for ourselves, to-day, any too ambitious titles, let us nevertheless assume so far as possible the philosophical and the religious attitude of mind; and in our inquiries of the former age let us seek for the causes which produced the peculiar and wonderful forms of life, both secular and spiritual, which we find originally in New England, in such communities as this one, and which, from these centres, have shaped the whole political and religious development of our land. We shall thus inevitably find ourselves assuming the attitude of mind most appropiate to such an occasion as this two hundredth anniversary, the attitude of *thanksgiving* and praise to God for the wonderful way in which he led our fathers, and for the wonderful blessings and opportunities which he has bestowed upon us.

In the first place, then, we may thank God, to-day, that the great constructive idea in the minds of our forefathers, as they came to the New England wilderness to establish for themselves homes and a government, was a *religious* idea.

Driven out of England in consequence of the zeal which they showed for a greater "scripture purity" in worship and doctrine than could be found in the Established Church; finding only a short rest at Amsterdam, and in Leyden, Holland, where they were "grieved with the corrupt examples around them, and fearing lest their children should be contaminated therewith," the Pilgrim Fathers set sail on August 5th, 1620, from Delft Haven, near Leyden, and in November of the same year landed on our bleak and wintry Massachusetts coast. They had left their homes, and endured the hardships of an uncertain and perilous sea-voyage to an unexplored and unknown land, *for a purpose;* and that purpose was that they might worship God according to the dictates of their own consciences and serve Him according to what seemed to them the scriptural and reasonable method, wholly unhindered by any ecclesiastical authority and unfettered by any popish forms.

The very foundations of our New England and national civilization were thus, in the providence of God, laid in religion. Coming here with this definite purpose of enjoying religious freedom, and of securing it, and its attendant blessings, to their posterity, the meeting house was the first thought and care of our fathers.

"In the settlements which grew up on the margin of the greenwood" says the historian Bancroft, "the plain meeting house of the congregation for public worship was everywhere the central point. Near it stood the public school by the side of the very broad road, over which wheels did not pass to do more than mark the path by ribbons in the sward. The snug farm houses, owned as freeholders, without quitrents, were dotted along the way, and the village pastor among his people, enjoying the calm raptures of devotion, 'appeared like such a little white flower as we see in the spring of the year, low and humble on the ground, standing peacefully and lovingly in the midst of the flowers round about; all in like manner opening their bosoms to drink in the light of the sun'. In every hand was the Bible; every home was a house of prayer; in every village all had been taught, many had comprehended a methodical theory of the divine purpose in creation, and of the destiny of man."

It is not difficult to trace the influence of this religious idea upon all departments of life in the growing communities in which our forefathers lived. Thus we can see that here was the starting point of that *educational system*, which has had so much to do with the making of the New England character, and which has given to New Englanders a worldwide reputation for intelligence, shrewdness, and common sense. The basis of the religion of our fathers was the

Bible. But to understand the Bible a certain amount of education was essential. Hence they forthwith established the necessary schools, that their children and the whole community might appreciate the arguments by which their religion was defended, and that an educated ministry might be furnished to lead them in divine things. "The Pilgrim Fathers well understood" says another, "that Protestant Christianity demands intellectual culture. The preaching of the gospel can only produce its best results when addressed to a people enjoying the advantages of some good measure of education." This they not only determined to furnish, but to make obligatory upon all. Here is the germ of our common school system. And it had its origin in the religious idea.

Again the whole political system, which secures freedom and equality to all our citizens, and which has proved such a stimulus to ambition, and such a conservator of justice and of peace, strikes its roots into identically the same ground. It was their profound conviction of the universal brotherhood and the absolute equality of the human race in the sight of God, that led our forefathers to remove from a land of tyranny to a land where they might enjoy the blessings of that freedom in which they believed. Their political institutions were the direct result of their religious ideas. The church and the state were identical. The meetings of the parish were the meetings of the town. To be entitled to a vote in political matters each person was required to become a member of some Congregational church. The historian, Bancroft, already quoted, says again: "*All New England* was an aggregate of organized democracies. But the complete development of the institution was to be found in Connecticut and the Massachusetts Bay. There each township was also substantially a territorial parish; the town was the religious congregation; the independent church was established by law; the minister was elected by the people who annually made grants for his support. * * He who will understand the political character of New England in the eighteenth century must study the constitution of its towns, its congregations, its schools and its Militia."

Once more this strong and clearly-defined religious idea of our ancestors made itself powerfully felt as a constructive force, in the building up, in the several communities, of a remarkable pure *moral* and *social* life. The influence of the church and the minister was everywhere strongly felt. Public sentiment was thus educated to condemn, almost harshly sometimes, whatever was impure and unholy in thought, word or deed. The transgressor was made to feel himself odious to the whole community, a blot upon its fair name and a disgrace to himself and all his friends. This popular disapproval thus became one of the very strongest possible deterrents from crime. It was popular to be religious, Sabbath-keeping was almost universal, Sabbath-breaking was scarcely known. In social customs whatever seemed to make for piety and seriousness was viewed with approval, and whatever interfered with a religious and devotional habit was sternly disapproved. Thus public opinion drew the line sharply between good and evil, and no one was left in doubt as to which he would be expected to choose.

So in all the departments of life, the religious idea of our forefathers made itself felt as a shaping and developing power, and to it we own all that is noblest and best in both the secular and religious institutions which have made our own New England, and indeed our whole country, what they are to day. We may well thank God that it was so grand a purpose and so noble a sentiment that drove our ancestors, so long ago, to this inhospitable coast, to found a State where education, liberty, and a pure religion might forever be the inalienable right of every citizen of the land.

I have dwelt thus far, dear friends, upon these general aspects of life in the time of our fathers, and upon the forces at work in the formation of society in their day, because it is only by knowing and recalling these things that we shall be prepared rightly to appreciate the part which this particular church has had in the conservation and application of these forces in this community in which we live.

I would mention then, in the second place, as a cause of devout thanksgiving and praise to God to-day, the fact that in His providence, this church has been permitted for two long centuries to exert so beneficent an influence, and to do so great a work in this town. What the religious idea of our forefathers did for New England as a whole, that, preeminently, this church, as the exponent of religion, has done in this community, in building up the intellectual, moral and political life of the place. I think we may say with perfect truthfulness and without boasting, that for two centuries this church has been the *chief* earthly means for securing the best blessings of God to the people of this town. As its meeting house stands conspicuous upon this hill, above the other buildings, so its influence has been preeminent among the good influences that have been working here. It has truly been as "a city that is set on an hill," and its light has not been hid.

It is not difficult to find illustrations of the beneficent and wholesome effect of this church and of its ministers upon the various departments of thought and life. Thus let us see what has been its influence in matters of *education* in this place.

"Our forefathers" says the historian of Essex[*], "were intelligent and well educated men. They knew therefore how to appreciate the importance of a good education for their children. But while in a wilderness, few and far between, and with scanty means of living, they could not build school houses and hire teachers and if they could have done it, the dangers from wild beasts would have rendered it hazardous

[*] History of Essex, p. 103 sq.

for their children to go and come from school. As late as 1723 wolves were so abundant and so near the meeting house that parents would not suffer their children to go and come from worship without some grown person. The education of their children however was not neglected. They were taught at home to read write and cipher, and were instructed in the great principles of religion, and in the principal laws of their country. And when in 1642 it was found that some parents were not faithful in these and other duties to their children, the Selectmen of the town were directed 'To see that children neglected by their parents are learned (so reads the record) to read and understand the principles of religion, and the capital laws of this country, and are engaged in some proper employment.' The same year the town voted that there should be a free school." These were the beginnings of education in this place. In 1651, thirteen years after the establishment of Harvard College, a Latin School was opened here to prepare young men for college, and in the next half century thirty eight went out from Ipswich and studied at Harvard. Eleven of these became ministers, three physicians, and the rest served in civil and judicial capacities.

Shortly after the founding of this church the people in this part of the town began to desire a free school for themselves. Heretofore they had been obliged to go for their schooling, as for their religious worship, to the further part of the town. A general meeting was therefore held in the meeting house, of all the voters in the parish, who, it must be remembered were all church members. The minister of the parish, Rev. Mr. Wise, is surposed to have been present and to have made an earnest address, exhorting his parishioners to "save their children from ignorance, infidelity and vice." The result of this meeting, which was thus due largely to the influence of the church, was the appointment of a committee to secure a teacher and a suitable room for a school. Nathaniel Rust, Jr. was chosen and he opened the school in his own house in June, 1695, and continued teaching for several years. The first school house was built in 1702. The school-masters were at this time, and for many years, chosen by the parish; and the parish was then nearly identical with the church.

From 1687 to 1715 the Ipswich grammar school was under the charge of Mr. Daniel Rogers, son of President Rogers, of Harvard College. During this period eight Chebacco boys were fitted for College in this school. their names were William Burnham, Benjamin Choate, Francis Cogswell, John Eveleth, Francis Goodhue, John Perkins, Henry and Jeremiah Wise. These names at once suggest to us that it was the ancestors of some of the principal families now living amongst us, who thus valued education and did all in their power to secure its blessing for themselves and their children after them. History has preserved for us a specimen[*] of the work of one of these Chebacco boys which will give us an idea of how the good people of that day estimated and used their advantages. In 1729 Rev. Jeremiah Wise, son of our first pastor, preached the election sermon in Boston, "before his Excellency, William Burnet, Esq, the honorable and Lieutenant-governor, the Council and representatives of the Provinces of the Massachusetts Bay." Among other things, the preacher said these words:

"The education of youth is a great benefit and service to the public. This is that which civilizes them, takes down their temper, tames the fierceness of their natures, forms their minds to virtue, learns them to carry it with a just deference to superiors, makes them tractable or manageable, and by learning and knowing what it is to be under government, they will know better how to govern others, when it comes to their turn. And thus it tends to good order in the State. Yea, good education tends to promote religion and reformation, as well as peace and order; as it gives check to

History of Essex, p. 147

idleness and ignorance, and the evil consequences thereof. Further by this means men are fitted for service, for public stations in Church and State, and to be public blessings. The public would greatly suffer by the neglect thereof, and religion could not subsist long but would decay and even die without it. The public weal depends upon it, and therefore it ought to be the public care, and so it has been in the best formed Commonwealths, who have erected and endowed public schools and colleges for the education of youth. This was our fathers early care, even in the infancy of the country, and their pious zeal for the glory of God and the good of their posterity has been remarkably blessed. Learning has flourished greatly under the care of the government, new colleges have been erected, and God has raised up generous friends to become benefactors to them."

The training that fitted our old pastor's son to make this earnest plan for enlarged views on the part of the "Civil Rulers" in regard to education, must have been given him in his Chebacco home and in the Chebacco church, and in the Ipswich School.

As the years go on, increasing attention is paid to education. In the early part of the present century the number of pupils in the three schools has increased to nearly three hundred, and each year the appropriations of money for school purposes show an increase over those of former years. As we turn the pages of the History of Essex, we meet with an ever enlarging number of names of those who went out from this parish to receive a liberal education, and to enter upon the professions and other higher walks of life. Exactly how much of this was due to the influence of the church, and to the wise counsel and instructions of its pastors, none can tell; but we may have the living testimony of a score or more liberally educated sons of Essex, who are to-day occupying important and influential positions in professional and business life, that the first quickening of the intellectual life within them, and the first impulses that impelled them toward a higher career were traceable directly to the teachings and personal influences of Crowell or Bacon or Choate. If this is true in the present it is safe to assume that it was equally true in the past. We may thank God to-day, for the large number of educated men that this church has given to the gospel ministry, and to the other useful and honorable professions in her day.

I cannot close this brief review of educational matters without alluding somewhat more particularly to the distinguished sevices and unique work in this department, of one who has probably had more to do with shaping the more recent intellectual life of the place than any other person, and whose influence can still be distinctly felt. I refer to the late Hon. David Choate. I am sure that our thanksgiving to-day must include a great deal of gratitude to God, for giving to the church, and to the town, a man who was fitted and disposed to do the work that this man did.

"For twenty seven years" says his biographer[*], "he engaged in his profession (of teaching) with a perseverance and enthusiasm that was marvellous. In the midst of that period he secured the erection of a new school building, and such a division and classification of pupils as enabled him to give to his own department at length the character and the curriculum of a high school. And that was at a time, be it remembered, when there were not more than a dozen high schools in the State. Here his power as an educator had freer scope, and was so marked and peculiar that no adequate idea of it can be given in few words. Through his energies, and personal influence with friends of learning, the school was provided with a library, a fine case of instruments for use in the study of natural philosophy, astronomy, and surveying, with outline maps, a piano and other appliances now common enough, but then rare indeed, if anywhere to be

[*] Rev. Prof. E. P. Crowell

found in the larger high schools. While courses of lectures on various branches of study were provided, the instruction itself was of a very high order. Hard study was indeed exacted of every scholar and each recitation was a searching test of the work done at one's desk or at home and of the pupils comprehension of the subject. Speaking of the school of another teacher, he once remarked: 'One great charm about the school was that the pupils were first brought up to as high a standard in close, hard study, in school and out, as they could be, and then made happy and cheerful in it'. But the excellence of Mr. Choate's school was not limited to this. No mechanical routine ever existed there, nor were the exercises of the daily sessions ever suffered to run in *ruts*. His pupils did not merely recite what they had learned from the text-book, but they were taught continually from the living lips. Whatever the lesson in hand it was his part to invest it for the whole class with a new interest, to let light in upon what was obscure, to go over the whole subject with explanation and comment and illustration, until it was fully understood and mastered by all. One of the distinguishing characteristics of his seminary might be said to be this direct contact of the mind of the teacher with that of the pupil as an inspiring quickening influence,— an electric force. He was fertile in expedients to excite a thirst for knowledge in the indolent, and an enthusiasm in the most sluggish, to secure steady application, and the independent and vigorous use of each one's own powers. One unique contrivance for effecting these most important ends was a 'general exercise' of half an hour every morning for the whole school, which usually consisted in a familiar lecture on some one of a great variety of topics distinct from, or supplementary to, the regular course of study, and which, abounding in facts of history and science and the arts, in aphorisms, biographical anecdotes, pratical suggestions as to habits of study, combined instruction and entertainment, and was admirably adapted to stimulate and enrich the minds of those who heard it. Often the members of the school were required to take notes of what was thus communicated orally, or to give the substance of it in writing in their own language. This indeed was but one of the many kinds of practice in composition, training in which was another prominent feature of the school, Mr. Choate being a firm believer in the saying of Bishop Jewell, which he would sometimes quote, that 'men gain more in knowledge by a frequent use of their pens than by the reading of many books'.

The fame of the school went into all that region round about. Scores of students were drawn in from different towns, in the vicinity and at a distance; there was an average number of members of about sixty; and never did the personality of a teacher more deeply impress itself upon his pupils. Horace Mann's remark was preeminently true of Mr. Choate as an instructor: 'The teachers influence is like that grade of ink which when first put upon paper is scarcely visible, but soon becomes blacker, and now so black that you may burn the paper on coals of fire, and the writing is seen in the cinders'."

I have made this somewhat extended quotation because it seemed appropiate to let another, who had known Mr. Choate personally and thoroughly, speak for him. As but recently a comparative stranger here, I can add my testimony to the great and permanent value of his influence, both in secular and religious education. That influence is still almost as really and distinctly felt by those who are working in the same lines of endeavor, as though he were still alive.

Turning now from these educational matters to the political life of this community in the past two centuries, we find the impress of the church to have been as marked and decided as we would expect to find it from what we know of the character of its men, and of the circumstances in which they lived. From the very beginning the founders and supporters of the church, were the founders and supporters of the town, and its ministers were actively engaged in civil and military affairs. I will confine myself to two or three incidents from the abundant materials that are ready at hand, for the illustration of this topic, in the expectation that others will give a more detailed account of facts.

Four years after the founding of the church, Sir Edmund Andros, the recently appointed Governor of all the New England Colonies, levied a tax upon the people of this colony, of 1d. on £1, which was in direct violation of their charter rights. The people of this town, under the lead of their minister, met together and "determined that it was not the duty of the town to aid in assessing and collecting this illegal and unconstitutional tax."* A general town meeting was addressed by Rev. Mr. Wise, who made "a bold and impressive speech in which he urged his townsmen to stand to their privileges, for they had a good God, and a good King to protect them." A report of this meeting was transmitted to the Council, as follows:

"At a legal town meeting, August 23, assembled by virtue of an order from John Usher, Esq. for choosing a commission to join with the Selectmen to address the inhabitants according to an act of his excellency the Governor, and Council, for laying of rates. The town then considering that this act doth infringe their liberty, as free English subjects of His Majesty, by interfering with the Statute Laws of the land, by which it was enacted that no taxes should be levied upon the subjects without the consent of an Assembly, chosen by the freeholders for assessing the same, they do therefore vote that they are not willing to choose a commissioner for such an end, without said privileges, and, moreover consent not that the Selectmen do proceed to lay any such rate, until it be appointed by a General Assembly, concurring with Governor and Council."

* History of Essex, p. 98.

As the result of this, Mr. Wise and five others, John Andrews, William Goodhue, Robert Kinsman, John Appleton and Thomas French, were arrested, carried to Boston and tried for "contempt and high misdemeanor." Mr. Wise was "suspended from the ministerial function, fined £50 and costs, and obliged to give a £1000 bond for good behavior for one year. The others were also heavily fined and disqualified for holding office. "The evidence in the case, as to the substance of it," says Mr. Wise, "was, that we too boldly endeavored to persuade ourselves we were Englishmen and under privileges, and that we were, all six of us aforesaid, at the town meeting of Ipswich aforesaid, and, as the witness supposed, we assented to the aforesaid vote, and, also, that John Wise made a speech at the same time, and said that we had a good God and a good King, and should do well to stand to our privileges." The town afterwards made up the loss to these defendants; and Mr. Wise brought an action against Chief Justice Dudley, who had denied him the privilege of *habeas corpus*, and recovered damages.

It has been written that "*The first man in America ever known to oppose the idea of taxation without representation, sleeps in the grave of the Rev. John Wise of Chebacco.*"

An interesting anecdote is related of Mr. Wise in his later days as follows:* On coming to church one Sunday morning the sad news is spread from neighbor to neighbor, that on the evening before a fishing boat arrived which had had a narrow escape from pirates in the Bay, and that the crew had seen these pirates capture a Chebacco boat and put several men aboard of her to convey her with the captured men, away to a distant port. This, of course, is an especial cause of anxiety to those who have friends at sea. In his prayer Mr. Wise "remembers all that are in danger, in perils by land in perils by sea, and prays especially for the deliverance of those neighbors and friends that had fallen into the hands of

* History of Essex, p. 133.

pirates. 'Great God,' he fervently cries, 'if there is no other way, may they rise and butcher their enemies,'— an expression long remembered, because the event showed that on that morning they rose upon the pirates and slew them, and thereby safely reached home."

The estimation in which Mr. Wise's public services were held while living, may be gathered from these words which were written at his death. "He was of a generous and public spirit; a great lover of his country, and our happy constitution; a studious assertor and faithful defender of its liberties and interests. He gave singular proof of this at a time when our Liberties and all things were in danger. And with undaunted courage he withstood the bold invasions that were made upon us. He was next called (in his own order) to accompany our forces in an unhappy expedition, where not only the pious discharge of his sacred office, but his heroic spirit; and martial skill, and wisdom did greatly distinguish him. * * * Upon the whole, justice and gratitude both oblige us to give him the Title of a Patron of his Country and a Father in Israel, and to join with an eminent minister in his publick mention of him that he was our Elijah, the Chariot of Israel, and the Horsemen thereof, our Glory and Defense."

The gradual encroachments of the English upon their liberties, which finally culminated in the war of the Revolution, were watched by our fathers with increasing excitement and indignation. When the news was received here that the cargoes of tea, which had arrived at Boston, had been thrown overboard in the harbor, they meet in town meeting, and voted:

"1. That the inhabitants of this town have received real pleasure and satisfaction from the noble and spirited exertions of their brethren of Boston, and other towns, to prevent the landing of the detested tea, lately arrived there from the East India Company, subject to duty which goes to support persons not friendly to the interests of this Province."

"2. That they highly disapprove of the consignees of the East India Company, because of their equivocal answers to a respectable committee of Boston, and their refusal to comply with the wish of their countrymen."

"3. That every person who shall import tea, while the act for duty on it continues, shall be held as an enemy."

"4. That no tea shall be sold in town while this act is in force; that if any one sell it here he shall be deemed an enemy."

"Voted that these resolves be sent to the committee of correspondence, of Boston."

The women of that day were as patriotic as the men and heartily cooperated in these efforts to resist the persistent invasion of their rights. In these exciting and critical times a most active part was taken by the fourth pastor of this church, the Rev. John Cleaveland.

An anecdote in the early experience of this man will give us an idea of his character, and also of the difference in some respects between the spirit of those times and of our own.

Shortly after entering Yale College at the age of 19, he went in vacation, in company with his parents and friends and a majority of the members of the church to which he belonged, to a meeting of the Separatists, and listened to the preaching of a lay-exhorter, or "new-light preacher," as the followers of Whitefield were called. Mr. Whitefield's methods were deemed "subversive of the established order of the churches," and on this account "were obnoxious to the government of Yale."

Upon his return after the vacation he was called before the faculty for the offence of having listened to this preaching, and upon his refusal to confess that he had done wrong, was expelled from college.

Years afterward his degree was conferred upon him by the college authorities, unsolicited, and his name was enrolled with the graduates of his class of 1745.

Mr. Cleaveland's voice was heard everywhere, in public and private, at the approach of the revolutionary struggle, urging his flock to stand firm, and to make any sacrifice for the cause of liberty. When the war fairly broke out he enlisted as Chaplain of Col. Little's regiment; "the 17th Foot, Continental Army." Says the historian of Essex:* "He practiced as he preached. It was remarked to the author by aged people forty years ago that Mr. Cleaveland preached all the men of his parish into the army and then went himself. Three of his four sons were in the service for a longer or shorter time. One of them, Nehemiah, enlisted in his sixteenth year, and served in the army investing Boston, and, at a later period, in New Jersey and at West Point. 'Not only by his professional services as Chaplain, but by various contributions to newspapers, he did much to encourage and further the great enterprise which had its issue in our national independence.'"

The same author relates this amusing anecdote of Mr. Cleaveland. "For the defence and protection of the coast of Cape Ann, a force of militia from the more inland towns was drafted, to be stationed there. On their march thither they passed through Chebacco, halted, and were paraded on the common, where they received their Chebacco fellow soldiers. On this occasion a prayer was offered by the ardent and patriotic Cleaveland. While he was praying in his stentorian voice "that the enemy might be blown"—"to hell and damnation," loudly interrupted an excited soldier,—"to the land of tyranny from whence they came," continued the undisturbed chaplain, without altering his tone or apparently noticing the interruption.

Bancroft mentions this old Chebacco pastor, as one of those Chaplains who preached, to the regiments of citizen-soldiers, a renewal of the days when Moses, with the rod of God in his hand, sent Joshua against Amalek."†

*History of Essex, p. 208. †History of U. S. Vol. IV: chap. 13.

In the war of the rebellion the ready responses of this town to the President's successive calls for troops, the patriotic sentiments heard here from all classes of citizens, and the bravery and endurance of the soldiers who went out to battle for the peace and good name of their country, show that, in later years, the old time ardor and public spirit had not died out.

It is the testimony of one who had much to do with the Essex men in the army* "that none were more prompt at the call of duty, none more obedient to commands, none made less complaint during the fatiguing march" than they.

But not only in times of war did the character and training of our citizens show itself. In times of peace, in seasons of quiet, every day experience, in the period of slow and almost imperceptible development, the influence of their traditions, the example of their ancestors, and the earnest utterances of this pulpit have been active forces that have given a decided character and value to the institutions and doings of the people of this town. These are things for which we cannot thank God too heartily, and of which we can hardly be too proud.

I have spoken, dear friends, of the influence of this church, as the exponent of the religious idea of our fathers, upon the intellectual and political life of this community. It remains for me to touch very briefly upon the part it has played in forming the social and moral life of the place. In their earliest days the various settlements and towns of New England were a good deal like large families. The people were thrown together and united by the circumstances in which they lived. Therefore it has been remarked that their social, civil, and ecclesiastical regulations resemble those which are adopted in every well-regulated family. It was the patriarchal stage in the history of our land. Under these circumstances, and with such men for their ministers as we have found the ministers of *our* fathers to have been, it is not surprising that the influence of the church and its pastors was very strongly felt

---

*Capt. Chas. Howes.

in the homes and in the hearts of all. Mr. Wise was "a tall, stout man, majestic in appearance, of great muscular strength," and with a voice "deep and strong." He was well calculated to inspire respect in the minds of his flock, for the house and the word and the laws of God. All the children were scrupulously instructed in the catechism. They were baptized in infancy and early taken to meeting on the Lord's day. Preparations for the Sabbath began on Saturday, and everything was done to secure the peace and quiet needed for devotion and spiritual rest. The Bible was read and respected in every home, and the father of the family opened and closed the labors of each day with family prayers. As we read of those simple and unostentatious homes we have a picture of pure and true domestic happiness such as is hardly afforded by any other age or country in the whole history of the world. And there went out from these quiet abodes of contentment and piety, noble men and women to do noble deeds and live noble lives.

The existence of Slavery in this town is mentioned in the year 1717, when it appears, by a bill of sale dated July 30, that "Joshua Norwood of Gloucester, sold to Jonathan Burnham of Chebacco, for £64 in bills of credit, a negro boy whom he had bought of Thomas Choate of Hogg Island." The modifying influences of our fathers' religious ideas upon this institution, and the circumstances that justified them in holding slaves at all, are thus brought out by Dr. Crowell in the history of the town.* "They did not send vessels to Africa to bring slaves to this country. They did not enter at all into the slave trade, nor willingly give it any encouragement. On the contrary they remonstrated most loudly against it. All the slaves here were originally brought from Africa to this country in English ships, and forced upon the colonies. 'England,' says Bancroft, 'stole from Africa, from 1700 to 1750 probably a million and a half of souls, of whom one-

*History of Essex, p. 124.

eighth were buried in the Atlantic, victims of the passage, and yet in England no general indignation rebuked the enormity. Massachusetts unremittingly opposed the introduction of slaves. In 1705 the General Court imposed a tax upon those who brought slaves into the market, of so much for every slave sold.' But England persisted in bringing them, and landing them upon our shores. But why did our fathers buy them? The only apparent reason is that of humanity or necessity. If they had not taken them into their families by purchase, they might have been left to perish in our streets, or subjected to all the horrors of another passage over the Atlantic, to be sold to some other country. If they had been unprovided for upon our shores, they must have perished; for they were as incapable of providing for themselves as the most neglected and ignorant child. Their condition, therefore, was at once improved, as soon as they came into the possession of our fathers. They dwelt under the same roof; their wants were all cared for; they worked shoulder to shoulder with their masters in the field; sat by the same fire with the children, were taken to church with them on the Sabbath, and instructed in the great truths of Christianity, and when our fathers were made free, they were made free with them. There is nothing in these facts to diminish aught of England's guilt in the enormities of the slave-trade; but they certainly furnish some apology for our fathers in giving a home to those who were already bondmen."

This town, under the lead of its ministers and religious men, was early identified with the temperance movement.

As early as in 1825 it was voted "that the selectmen allow no bills for liquor on the highway." On the 16th of July, 1829, the first public address upon this subject in this town, was delivered in the meeting house of this church, by William C. Goodell, of Boston. The speaker announced his topic as follows: "Ardent spirits ought to be banished from the land. What ought to be done can be done." The result of the lecture was the formation, then and there, of the first temperance society. It was called the "Essex Temperance Society on the principle of total abstinence," and the constitution was drawn up by the lecturer and the pastor of this church. Seven persons joined the society and signed the pledge that evening. Their names were Winthrop Low, Samuel Burnham, John Choate, John Perkins, Jonathan Eveleth, Francis Burnham, David Choate. Rev. Mr. Crowell's name was added shortly afterward.

It is pleasant to add that, from the first, whenever the question of licensing the sale of intoxicating liquor has come up in the annual meetings of the town, it has received a decided *negative*, up to, and including, the present year.

I have said nothing at all *directly* dear friends, about the influence of this church in distinctively religious and ecclesiastial affairs. Had it been my object to give a connected and comprehensive history of the society, that would have been the principal topic. And it would have been a very rich one. Not that in this or in any of the things that I *have* mentioned, this church has been *perfect*. Not that she has not committed errors of judgment and made mistakes. There are things in the past that we may wish were different. But in the main, by the grace of God, she has made a noble record, not only in the development and preservation of piety and the graces of the Christian life here at home; but also in her contributions to Christian literature (especially in the works of Wise and Cleaveland); in her not inconsiderable influence in founding and aiding other churches in this county; in her collections and prayers for foreign missions; and in the noble *men* she has sent out in such considerable numbers, to become earnest and able preachers of Jesus Christ.

These things you will hear about from others. But after all that I have said, and after all that they shall say has been uttered, to the praise of God, and to the credit of our noble ancestry, the very richest and best of these past two centuries will still be unuttered and unutterable. These things that we can see and speak of, these visible and tangible results, are glorious, and we thank God for them; but who can estimate the invisible influences and the untraceable forces that have been operating in all these years through the instrumentality of this church and her pastors! The best work accomplished by any church and in any pastorate consists in the *thought* that is stimulated, the *spiritual impressions* that are imparted, the *hopes* and *desires* that are enkindled in the soul. These lead the soul heavenward. And who shall number, to-day the souls that have been cheered and guided in their earthly journey, by these influences, and that have been won to Christ and made heirs of everlasting life through the instrumentality of this ancient church? We may seem to see them now, a joyous and blessed band, in the great company of those who have washed their robes and made them white in the blood of the Lamb. Our fathers and brethren, our neighbors and kindred, our acquaintances and friends are there. And do they not see us? Yea we must believe that this sanctuary is still sacred to them, and that these memories that we are reviving are *their* memories. They are *with* us to-day, uniting in our thanksgiving and joining in our praises to that God and that Christ who have made this sacred church to be to so many, as the very gate of heaven. God grant that we may triumph as they have triumphed, over all the hinderances and temptations and doubts that assail us, and enter with them at last *through* this gate, and *into* the blessedness of that heavenly land.

Finally, as we stand, to-day, upon the vantage-ground of this two hundredth anniversary, we can look *forward* as well as backward. Someone has said that to know any leading characteristic virtue of those from whom we have descended is not only to be influenced by it, but it is to be put under an obligation to imitate it, and keep it alive. Mediæval knights committed to memory the records of noble acts in their families, that they might maintain an equally high standard by their own chivalric deeds. So we are put upon our honor to maintain the high principles and to imitate the noble achievements of those who have gone before us. This anniversary should be full of measureless edification and inspiration for us. It should arouse us to new earnestness and activity. We should feel as never before the vast opportunities and solemn responsibilities that are ours. As we thank God for the past we should *pray* to him for the future. New problems confront us. The world has marvellously changed since the days of our fathers. The ends of the earth are given into our keeping. Shall we keep them *for Jesus?* The most diverse race elements, with the utmost variety of religious and political and social prejudices, are pouring into our own nation. Shall the gospel permeate these masses? Shall it be the *light* of the world, the *salt* to save the people from corruption and decay? With us rests the issue. Intemperance and licensiousness, those old enemies, still stalk about the land. Shall we kill them with the sword of law and of love? Mammon is as greedy as ever. Worldliness still draws its millions from the worship and service of God. It is ours to apply the gospel with its quickening and purifying and saving power to all within the reach of our influence; and by the wonderful discoveries of modern times, God has brought the *whole world* within our influence. The church of to-day needs the entire energy and complete consecration of all its members. As we remember the deeds of our ancestors let us then, not be rendered proud and self satisfied by them, but let us be spurred on to new faithfulness to the trusts that devolve upon us. Let us determine to show the same spirit in meeting our responsibilities that they showed in meeting theirs. If we have different difficulties to contend with and different problems to solve, let us rejoice that we have the *same gospel* to work with, and the *same Saviour* for our helper and friend. Let us ever be true to that Saviour. Let us ever be loyal to this church and its covenant. Let us ever maintain these same grand old evangelical doctrines, that in the past have brought forth, in abundance, such goodly fruitage. Let us contribute liberally and gladly to the support of the gospel, upon which rest the eternal hopes of man. Let us be *personally* interested and faithful to all these responsibilities; and then that light, which so long ago was kindled on this sacred hill, shall continue to shine, to warm and to bless men. Long after we have left the scenes of earth and gone to join that great company of the redeemed, we shall be remembered, as we remember our ancestors to-day; and to God the Father and to the Lord Jesus shall be the praise and the glory forever. Amen.

Historical Discourse

BY PROF. H. E. CROSBY.

While towns and colleges are making special observance of the fiftieth anniversary of their foundation, and the whole country has ever since 1874 been passing through a series of centennial celebrations of momentous political events, — reaching this very year that of the treaty of peace with Great Britain and the disbanding of the Revolutionary Army, — we certainly, Respected Friends, have no occasion to apologize for this assembling to-day to pay such regard as we may to an occurrence of so much greater antiquity, the planting in this community, two centuries ago, of this church and parish, which have been living on, the centre and spring of the religious and almost of the secular life of this people during these two hundred years.

You do not need to be reminded that it is now ninety years and more since the frame of the present church edifice (which is the fourth), with its oaken posts, was raised on the spot, which forty years earlier than that, had, at the erection of the third church building, been consecrated to the worship of God, and which has, ever since 1752, been known as meeting-house hill.

As lately as 1864 the location and ground-plan of the second meeting-house, erected in 1718, near the site of the present town pound, were marked perfectly by the underpinning stones.

remaining for all that intervening period a memorial—like the twelve stones taken out of Jordan, and pitched in Gilgal— of the place where were manifested the power and grace of the Lord toward us in the earlier years of the eighteenth century.

But for the event we are now commemorating our thoughts must ascend past all these intermediate stages of this parochial history, beyond everything that has taken place in the life of the nation and the province, to a point within the limits of the earliest colonial period, when, in the first meeting-house, built three years before, at the North End, near the site of the house and barns of Mr. Nehemiah Dodge, this church was constituted, and the Rev. John Wise ordained its pastor on the 12th of August (O. S.) in the year 1683.

The mere fact that our church and parish have reached so venerable an age is however the least of our reasons for observing this bi-centennial. These special services in honor of this birthday are made in the highest degree becoming because of the qualities and the doings of the ministers and the laymen of this Religious Society in all the past. Because of its vigorous life and its beneficient career in every generation from the beginning until now, it is meet and our bounden duty to consider these years of many generations, as one epoch now closes, and we stand on the threshold of another.

Through tradition and the printed page* you are well acquainted with this chapter of church and parish history, and there is no need, if there were time, of my undertaking to tell the whole story, full of interest as it is. I only ask you to review with me three passages in this history, which perhaps best illustrate what these twin institutions have been, the changes they have passed through and the work they

---

*History of the Town of Essex from 1634 to 1868 by the late Rev. Robert Crowell D. D., Pastor of the Congregational Church in Essex. Essex: Published by the Town, 1868.

have done, and which may therefore most suitably be recalled to our thoughts, and accounted most worthy of permanent remembrance.

1. The first of these passages is, of course, that which describes the circumstances of the founding of this Ecclesiastical body.

If then we inquire what it was which brought about the establishment of this church and parish, we cannot fail to find the real cause and the explanation in the character of the people of Chebacco — their piety, their intelligence, and their force of will combined.

You recollect that the great current of emigration from England, beginning in 1620 and bringing to these shores some twenty thousand souls, had nearly ceased to flow about forty years before the time to which we are now turning our attention; and though not a few of the first settlers were still living, a large proportion of the inhabitants here were now, in 1683, Englishmen of the second generation, many of them, to be sure, born in the mother country. Their fathers had come bringing them from various parts of the ancestral land; from Bristol in the southwest, on the banks of the Avon, through which Wyckliffe's ashes had flowed to the sea; from the flourishing cathedral city of Norwich, the capital of Norfolk county on the east coast, where in 1580 (as our highest authority on the history of Congregationalism has told us,) by the prompting and under the guidance of Robert Browne, the first church in modern days had been formed, which was intelligently Congregational in its platform and processes; from old Ipswich also, the capital of Suffolk county, noted as the birth-place of Cardinal Wolsey and for its Grammar School, revived by him, though founded in the reign of Edward the Fourth; and from various smaller villages in its vicinity, such as Groton, the old home of Governor Winthrop.

And these new-world founders were of the very choicest fruit of the Protestant reformation. The dwellers in Chebacco between the years 1676 and 1683 were thus of the bone and sinew of a town of which Edward Johnson, an author of the seventeenth century, in his History of New England, said: "The peopling of Ipswich is by men of good rank and quality, many of them having the revenue of large lands in England, before they came to this country;" and of which Cotton Mather, in 1638, declared: "Here was a renowned church consisting of such illuminated christians, that their pastors, in the exercise of their ministry, might think that they had to do, not so much with disciples as with judges."

These Chebacco residents were the sons and daughters of the original occupants of a territory, of which, in common with all those settled in Massachusetts Bay, a recent writer has remarked that "there was in the early emigration to this region, besides the educated Puritan clergymen, quite another admixture than that of learning, a sturdy yeomanry, led hither by the desire to better its condition and create a new religious world around it."

These our ancestors of two hundred years ago were among the freemen of a body politic, of which, what Rev. William Stoughton said in his election sermon in 1668 of *all* New England was preeminently true, that "God sifted a whole nation that he might send choice grain into this wilderness."

The men and women who proposed to themselves the founding of this church, belonged to a municipality where already for forty-one years there had been a free school, and a standing town rule that the selectmen should see that no child fail to be taught reading and the principles of religion and the capital laws of the country; where for thirty-two years there had been an endowed Grammar School, at which some thirty-five boys had already been fitted for Harvard College.

Not only had the town of Ipswich, of which Chebacco was an integral part, thus laid a foundation for the intelligence and virtue of all within its borders, as well as reproduced the local civil institutions of the old country and aided in setting up the fabric of a State government, but it was now, according to the historian Palfrey, "the second town in the colony in importance, having a larger degree of talent and intelligence than almost any other," and in King Philip's war, (i.e. 1675) "one of the centres of intelligence, of whose church several of the officers and many of the troops, who did good service, were members." And it was also now experiencing to the full the stimulating and developing effect of the political agitations of all that formative period.

In the contests between the crown and the colony over the civil rights claimed by the latter, which had been almost continually going on throughout the reigns of the first and second Charles, intermitted only during the few years of the ascendancy of Cromwell and the Commonwealth, and which were to terminate with the unrighteous taking away of the colonial charter, the very next year, 1684, by Charles the second, the citizens of this as well as of the other parts of Ipswich were as deeply interested spectators or participants, as any of you were in the war of the rebellion, or in the state and Federal election campaigns which have taken place since. And largely by these experiences were their mental powers made acute, their love of liberty inflamed, their manhood moulded and disciplined.

The church at Ipswich centre which was now about a half-century old, founded in May, 1634, the year of the settlement of Chebacco, had been first under the ministrations of Rev. Nathaniel Ward of Cambridge University and formerly a lawyer in England, of so acute and vigorous a mind, and so learned in jurisprudence that he was appointed by the civil authorities to compose the earliest statute code of the colony —the one hundred fundamental laws styled the "Body of Liberties"—which Palfrey calls a great monument of his wisdom and learning, and which he says will compare favorably with other works of its class in any age.

Its ministers, during the childhood and youth of those in Chebacco now in mature life, had been the colleagues John Norton of the same English University, also distinguished for learning and for his stirring eloquence, who took a leading part in the synod which constructed the Cambridge platform of faith and discipline in 1648, and Nathaniel Rogers, also an English University man, whom Cotton Mather, in 1702, called *the Holy* and regarded as "one of the greatest divines that ever set foot upon the American strand."

For nearly the thirty years (prior to 1683) during which the Chebacco people who were to embark in this new enterprise had been on the stage of active life, the religious welfare of Ipswich had been nominally cared for by three spiritual guides at once. One of them, the venerable Thomas Cobbet, educated at Oxford, driven for conscience sake to the new world, who through his talents, erudition and skill as a writer and theologian had stood in the foremost rank of New England divines, was now, to be sure, at the infirm age of seventy-five.

The second, John Rogers, a son of Rev. Nathaniel, was rather in the position of an assistant, having charge of the Thursday lecture, and chiefly absorbed in his other profession as the principal physician of the town—a scholar and a scientist, elected President of Harvard College, and inaugurated to that office, it so happened, the very day this Chebacco church was constituted. But the third of these colleagues in the pastoral office, the Rev. William Hubbard, born in England, but a graduate of Harvard, regarded by a contemporary historian as "certainly for many years the most eminent minister in the county of Essex, equal to any in the Province for learning and candor, and superior to all his contemporaries as a writer," described from other contemporary allusions "as a stately, affable and accomplished gentleman, the ideal country pastor in a highly intellectual community," was precisely at this juncture in the mature vigor of manhood, and active and influential in all the ecclesiastical affairs of the whole town.

These statements may be sufficient to remind us what were the antecedents and the political training, and what the educational and religious privileges of our fathers, who took into serious consideration the spiritual interests and needs of this growing and thriving precinct of Ipswich, at their first meeting for consultation on that subject, at the house of William Cogswell, a little north of the site of Mr. Albert Cogswell's, in February, 1677.

Their character, then, admirably qualified them for entering on this great and good work. But who actually took the initiative in it? Was it these associate pastors at the centre? By no manner of means. We discover not a trace of their ever holding preaching services in this remote but populous part of the town, or of their taking any measures for the establishment of stated religious worship here, or of their even encouraging any movement in that direction. There seems to have been on their part a most singular inaction and an indifference to the spiritual welfare of this large part of their flock, all the more strange because Prince's *Christian History* tells us that "a gradual decline of religion and morals grew very visible and threatening as early as 1670 and was generally complained of and bitterly bewailed by the pious; and yet much more in 1680." Was it really indifference? Felt's *History of Ipswich* makes the unconsciously sarcastic statement that in 1677 "Rev. Mr. Hubbard was *tried*, in having a part of his people at Chebacco much engaged in endeavors to have Mr. Jeremiah Shepard for their minister; his chief objection being that Mr. Shepard had not become a member of any church." Indeed! Then he did have *other* objections, also. And this little piece of evidence is sufficient to prove that Mr. Hubbard's position as to this project was not one of support or approval.

When the historian Palfrey gives us some insight into his

character in the declaration that "Hubbard took no generous part in the great political struggles of his time, and that the tone of his *History of New England* is courtly and timid;" when we hear not a syllable of remonstrance from this Ipswich minister in unison with the outspoken opposition of his fellow-townsmen to Governor Andros' tyranny in 1687, and learn that he was appointed by that governor the acting president of Harvard College in 1688, we cannot but infer that such a man sided with his parishioners at the centre, in positive opposition to the loss of so much taxable property, from his parish, as would be caused by the creation of another parish at Chebacco.

At any rate it is plain that without the counsel or sanction, without the help or sympathy of their spiritual advisers, the movement for the founding of this church and parish began with the residents of this village themselves, from their own deep sense of the value and the need of better religious privileges for all in their community. Recall their own statement of the reasons for their acting in this matter, and of the motive which inspired them.

The record reads: "At this [the first] meeting, the inhabitants of Chebacco, considering the great straits they were in for want of the means of grace among themselves;" and: "that we might obtain the ministry of the word among ourselves, which is our heart's desire;" and further: "that we might be eased of our long and tiresome Sabbath days' journeys to the place of public worship in our town; for some hundreds of our inhabitants do not nor with convenience can attend the public worship at town; and of so considerable a number of the inhabitants as are amongst us, scarce fifty persons the year throughout do attend the public worship of God on the Sabbath days." And their first petition to the General Court, June 1, 1677, mentions, as a reason for having liberty to build a meeting house, their desire "to prevent the profanation of the Sabbath, they living so remote."

Several things in their movement are worthy of particular notice, for a full appreciation of what these men were and what they accomplished.

One is their respect for authority, their careful conformity to existing requirements in ecclesiastical as well as civil affairs, the law-loving and law-abiding spirit manifest in them, saddled though they were with the burden of helping to support three ministers at once, without being permitted to have the preaching services of either of them, even in the winter, and deeply conscious that the management of their own religious affairs by themselves and for themselves was a part of their inalienable rights.

Another is the clear, logical, masterly way in which they present and maintain their cause before the General Court, in what they call "A declaration and vindication of the transactions of the inhabitants of Chebacco in the precincts of Ipswich, in reference to their late proceedings in obtaining the ministry of the Gospel among them." I presume you are all familiar with this remarkable document; but I cannot refrain from quoting their statement of a few of the arguments and the charges Ipswich had brought against them, and the points they so aptly make in reply:

"1. They [The Ipswich selectmen] alleged that the war was not yet past, and God's judgments were yet hanging over us, and the town was at great charge; to which we replied that when we sought to have the means of grace amongst ourselves, we looked at it as our duty; and therefore, when the judgments of God were amongst us, that it was rather an argument to stir us up to our duty than to lie under the omission of it; neither would we put the town to charge, either to erect our meeting-house, or maintain our minister."

"3. They alleged we belonged to the town, and therefore, were obliged to help the town to bear the charges, and they could not spare our money; to which we replied that they alleged, at the General Court, that we paid only 17 or 18 pounds to the ministers of Ipswich; and there were three ministers to whom the town paid 200 pounds per annum; and if the town would supply us with one of them, we would pay one of them fifty pounds toward his maintenance yearly. Then they replied, that could not be; and that our want was only in the winter, and if we could get a minister to preach to us in the winter, they would free us from paying to the minister in the town, in the winter season; and we should come to the public worship in the town in the summer, and pay there. We put ourselves in a posture for the entertaining the gospel, and were willing to lay aside our self-interests, that we might build a house for the worship of God, which we were the more vigorous in, by reason that we had experienced much, in a little time, of the sweetness and good of that privilege in enjoying the means amongst ourselves, whereby the generality of our inhabitants could comfortably attend the public worship of God. The house that we have been busied about for this place of public worship, we ever intended for such an end, always with this provisal, that this Honored Court do authorise the same, or countenance our proceedings therein; if not, we shall ever own ourselves loyal subjects to authority; and therefore, the same is erected upon a propriety, that if this Honored Court see not meet to favor our proceedings, we may turn our labors to our best advantage. These things we desire to leave with this Honored Court, as a declaration of our cause, and a vindication of our innocency, and are ready further to inform this Honored Court, in what they may please to demand, or in what may be alleged against our proceedings."

A third thing worthy of notice in these proceedings is the deliberateness with which they set themselves at work, the skilful measures they adopted and the indomitable perseverance they exercised in overcoming the obstacles which in succession blocked their way at every step. At their first meeting, in February, 1677, the inhabitants of Chebacco unanimously drew up a petition and soon after presented it to the town, desiring liberty to call a minister to preach among themselves. This the town neither granted nor denied, but would not vote upon it. Chebacco then petitioned the General Court, only to be referred back (June 1, 1677) to the town; which by direction of the Court made answer at the next session of that body in October. But even then, the Legislature, "considering what was alleged by Ipswich," would only "judge it not meet to grant the petition *at present*"; but seriously commended it to the town "to contrive as soon as may be for the accomodation of the petitioners." By vote of the town, March 2, 1678, the Selectmen held several conferences with the Chebacco leaders but without any result. The latter next asked leave to invite Mr. Jeremiah Shepard to preach to them,

to which none of the town fathers objected and some of them
assented. After he had preached a few Sabbaths beginning
with January 19, 1679, there was an intimation "from an honorable brother" at the centre, that the church were dissatisfied
with the proceedings here, and so he ceased preaching. February 4, a second petition was presented to the town, the only
effect of which was that the town sent to the General Court.
March 15, a petition and address with grave charges against
Chebacco.

"Not long after this," as the records tell us, "the sills of
the meeting-house were laid in Mr. William Cogswell's land
and the timber in place ready to raise. While we were in this
great conflict, that all things seemed to act against us, some
women, without the knowledge of their husbands, and with
the advice of some men, went to other towns and got help
and raised that house that we had intended for a meeting-
house, if we could get liberty."

This was the heinous offence for which Mrs. William Goodhue,
Mrs. Thomas Varney, and Mrs. Abraham Martin were arrested,
tried in Ipswich, found guilty of contempt of authority and
bound over to the next Court in Salem. Although this transaction complicated matters still more and somewhat embar-
rassed the Chebacco fathers and husbands, they went on with
the preparation of the "Declaration of their cause and Vindication of their innocency," and duly submitted the document
to the General Court, which on the 28th of May (1679) passed
an order, which together with the action of the committee
appointed by it is to be considered as the act of incorporation
or charter of the Parish.*

And so in April 1680 the house is dedicated, and in response to their call and by leave of the Great and General
Court, Mr. Wise begins his preaching in it. It was not, however, until February of the next year, 1681, that the people
were released from taxation for the support of the ministry

* See Appendix A.

at the centre; and although the church members living in Chebacco made request, September 6, 1681, for dismission from the mother church, in order to organize the new one, they were unable to obtain release from its bonds for nearly two years more.

With such steady persistence did these children of the Puritans, engrossed though they were with the work of the farm, the mill, the shop, the ship-yard and the fishery, push on this most noble and laudable project, for six long years, until their efforts were crowned with complete success.

When you look carefully over their doings and read their own plain and methodical statement of the facts in the case, entered upon their records for permanent preservation and the knowledge of their posterity, you know not which most to admire, in your survey of this protracted contest, the unconquerable determination of Englishmen to gain full possession of their religious rights, for the enjoyment of which they had been brought, from a land of plenty they could see no more, into all the hardships and privations of the new world, and to leave "unstained what there they found,—freedom to worship God" as their consciences dictated—or the shrewdness and the skill with which these, by no means "rude forefathers of the hamlet" pressed their rightful claim to a meeting-house and a minister of their own, to a triumphant conclusion on that 12th of August, 1683; when in that crowded audience-room, this church of Christ was organized, the covenant entered into and Mr. Wise formally set apart to the work of the gospel ministry and the pastoral care of Chebacco parish.

Consider, further, who the individual leaders in this matters were,—known to us, as they are in part, through their descendants.

The first committee of conference with the Ipswich selectmen, were William Cogswell, then about sixty-four years of age, John Andrews, Senior, sixty, Thomas Low, fifty-one, and

William Goodhue, forty-three. Two of these, Cogswell and Andrews, were also on the committee of four, who acted for the church at its organization, and are the only ones mentioned by name, of its original members. A third on that organizing committee was William Story, aged sixty-nine, and the fourth was John Burnham, sixty-seven, one of the first two deacons. John Choate, at this time a young man of twenty-two, later on in the first pastorate, also held the office of deacon. These men we may then reasonably regard as the seven pillars in this new structure.

William Cogswell was a descendant of Lord Humphrey Cogswell, whose coat of arms dated from the year 1447, and was one of the three sons of the wealthy merchant, John Cogswell, a passenger in the ship *Angel Gabriel*, and the progenitor of all of that name in this town. One of William's great-grandsons, Jonathan Cogswell, was also a deacon from 1780 until his death in 1812, at the age of eighty-six; and another, Col. Jonathan Cogswell, who died in 1819, was an officer in the Revolution. From William's brother John have descended two of your bi-centennial committee — one of them a deacon for twenty-one years already.

John Andrews, Sen., a freeman of Ipswich in 1642, was one of the six who joined Mr. Wise in that preparatory caucus at the centre four years later (Aug. 22, 1687), where, according to a reliable reporter, "they discoursed and concluded that it was not the town's duty anyway, to assist that ill method of raising money, which Sir Edmund Andros had ordered, without a general assembly;" and in his resistance in town meeting the next day, to this attempted illegal taxation, which, as the vote of Ipswich declared, "doth infringe their liberty as free-born English subjects of His Majesty." With the others, Mr. Andrews was arrested, denied the writ of habeas corpus, imprisoned in Boston, by a packed jury — principally strangers and foreigners — found guilty of contempt and high misdemeanor, made ineligible for office, fined

£30 and costs, and put under bonds of £500. From Mr. Andrews have descended all of that name in town, among them his grandson, John Andrews, a deacon in the church for many years until his death in 1750, and the late Col. William Andrews, a man who was said to have filled many offices of trust and honor in town with singular zeal and fidelity.

There is good reason also for believing that this John Andrews, Sen., was a son of the Captain Andrews, who commanded the ship *Angel Gabriel* on the voyage when she was wrecked on the coast of Maine, and who was the uncle of the boys John and Thomas—sons of Robert and Mary (Andrews) Burnham of Norwich, Eng.— sailing to this country under his charge and (with another brother) the ancestors of all that wide-spread and numerous family. This John Burnham, who was one of the first deacons, was the grandfather of a John Burnham who was deacon from 1732, till his death in 1746, and the great grandfather of Thomas Burnham, a deacon thirty-four years from 1765 to 1799, who for many years lined the psalm and set the tune in Church, and was also a school teacher. Among others of his descendants, were Maj. John Burnham, who served in the Continental Army throughout the Revolutionary war, styled by his Colonel, (afterwards Gov. Brooks) "one of the best disciplinarians and most gallant officers of the Revolution," a member of the church here for many years until his removal to Derry, N.H., in 1798, where he died in 1843 aged 94; and Maj. John's brother Samuel, a man of sterling worth and a leading citizen throughout a long life in Dunbarton, N. H., to which he removed about 1765. Four of his sons and sixteen others of his descendants were graduates of Colleges. From the brother of Dea. John Burnham also descended the four deacons of this name in the present century.

From that same town of Norwich, England, came also in 1637, William Story, a carpenter, one of this committee of conference with the selectmen, and one of the original church members. His son, Seth Story, was a deacon from 1694 till his death in 1732. His grandson, Seth Story, was a deacon and afterwards a ruling elder, until his death in 1786 at the age of ninty-three; and his grandson, Zechariah Story, was a deacon forty-four years until his death in 1774, at the age of ninety. They were both farmers and lived at the Falls, near the spot where now stands the house of Mr. Adoniram Story. Of this Dea. Zechariah Story, a daughter, Deborah, a true mother in Israel, married Wesley Burnham, and lived to the age of ninety-eight; and the children of one of her sons (Wesley Burnham, 2d), were Molly, Nathan, Asa, Michael, Henry, Anne, Samuel, Richard, Ruth and Wesley Burnham 3d; and the wife of *this* Wesley was Hannah a granddaughter of that same Elder Seth Story and the mother of seven children, whom you have well known as active and useful members of this church, within a generation.

From a brother of William Story have descended the rest of the name in this place, of whom I can only mention, because of their prominence in parish affairs, or of their connection with the history of this Church,—William Story, a merchant in Boston, a leading man in the Separatist Society there in 1746, and a delegate from it on the Council which organized the Separate church here that year, some of whose letters, still preserved written in a clear, beautiful hand, and well expressed, indicate a degree of culture beyond the average of that time; "Master" Joseph Story, a Revolutionary soldier, a school teacher for thirty years and parish clerk for a long period; and Esq. Jonathan Story, the able and impartial magistrate, the influential and useful citizen of the present century, often holding offices in the parish.

Dea. Thomas Low, (a son of the first settler of that name in Ipswich and a grandson of Capt. John Low, commander of the ship *Ambrose* and acting rear-admiral of a fleet of twelve ships sailing to Salem in 1630,) was born in 1632, was a deacon from 1683 until his death in 1712, for several years was parish clerk, and prominent in all the affairs of the community. It is on land which he owned, and near his homestead that we are gathered to-day. Among his descendants have been Lieut. Stephen Low, killed in battle in the French and Indian war; Major Caleb Low and Capt. David Low, soldiers of the Revolution; and of this century Capt. Winthrop Low, the first one to rise to take the pledge, when volunteers were called for, after the first temperance address here, in 1829, "a consistent, liberal supporter of the institutions of religion" and fully and heartily identified with all the interests of the parish, as one of its most influential and wealthy members.

William Goodhue, the fourth on the conference committee, (a son of William Goodhue, freeman of Ipswich, in 1636, who was said to have been one of the most influential men in the colony of Massachusetts, conferring honor upon his name and family by his many virtues), married Hannah, an Ipswich girl, a daughter of Rev. Francis Dane, afterwards of Andover. She was one of the three wide awake, fearless and energetic women, who committed the enormous crime of procuring or abetting the raising of a meeting-house in Chebacco. As this affair attests, she was well matched with her husband, who, believing with his pastor that "we have a good God and a good King, and should do well to stand on our privileges," shared with Mr. Wise and Mr. Andrews the glory of imprisonment and fine by Andros, and as the historian, Pitkin says of him, and his associates, "may justly claim a distinguished rank among the patriots of America." Mr. Goodhue was one of the selectmen, and a representative at several different times, was a deacon in the church, a leading man in the parish, and was "highly respected, eminently useful and greatly beloved." Taking into consideration the fact that he was the only one of the seven who was just then in the early prime of manhood, it can hardly be doubted that he composed that able memorial, the "Declaration and Vindication of the transactions of the people of Chebacco." One of Dea.

Goodhue's sons was Rev. Francis Goodhue who graduated at Harvard College, in 1699, and was pastor of a church in Jamaica, L. I.; and a descendant of his brother is now in the same office of deacon here.

John Choate, the last of the early deacons, the eldest son of the first settler of that name, and grandson of Goodman Choate of Groton, England, (a friend of Gov. Winthrop), was born in 1661, and was an office-bearer in the church from 1712 till his death in 1733. It was his granddaughter, the wife of Gen. Michael Farley who sent three sons into the Revolutionary Army, and when the youngest of them, a boy of sixteen, was about to start for the seat of war, "charged him to behave like a man;" and who, on a sudden call for ammunition for a company marching on short notice, with her own hands filled their powder horns from a barrel of powder in the attic of her house. John's brother Benjamin was a graduate of Harvard in 1703, and a pastor at Kingston, N. H. One of his nephews, whose name was also John, was a man of great ability and eminence in public life from 1731 until his death in 1766, as Judge of Probate and of the Court of Common Pleas, Executive councillor, Speaker of the House of Representatives, and Col. of the 8th Mass. regiment and Judge Advocate General in Pepperell's successful expedition against Louisbourg in 1745. Another was Francis, a ruling elder in the church for thirty-one years until his death in 1777, and the great grandfather of Dea. David Choate and Hon. Rufus Choate. A grand-nephew of Dea. John Choate, Hon. Stephen Choate was also a deacon from 1765 to 1783.

What and where, but for these seven men, we might well ask, would be this virtuous, well-instructed and prosperous community to-day?

Not by direction of any church authorities were these religious institutions planted in that early time on this ground; but by the enlightened piety, and the resolute temper of individual laymen, animated by a common spirit, and unselfishly seeking the highest welfare of the whole people, whose representatives and leaders were these our seven heroes, these heads of our tribes, William Cogswell, John Andrews, John Burnham, William Story, Thomas Low, William Goodhue, John Choate, the master-workmen in the rearing of the goodly walls of this our Zion, upon the foundation of the apostles and prophets, Jesus Christ himself being the chief cornerstone. It was their qualities of character, the inherited intelligence, the sense of duty, the godly zeal, and the tenacity of purpose of these Englishmen of the second generation, quickened, developed, made stalwart by their long discipline in a school of trying experiences, that created this twin organization of church and parish on this territory. And therefore let their names be held in highest honor and in everlasting remembrance. Aye, and they shall be. This ecclesiastical structure is of itself their ever-during monument, for they "builded better than they knew," and through the permanence of its strength and beauty, though dying, behold they live. We think of them, as "each in his narrow cell forever laid" in yonder ancient grave-yard, which they had, just about that time, set apart and put in order,—we say of them that they, like all the dead, "forgotten lie, alike unknowing and unknown," but in their work their name liveth evermore. It is no slight testimony to the intelligence of these men, that in their search for a minister for Chebacco, they discerned the worth of such a man as Mr. Wise, and by no means the least of their services to religion that they selected and secured him for their pastor. The special address to be presently given on this occasion upon his life, pastorate and character, renders unnecessary any mention of this eminent theologian and patriot here.

It is a matter of some interest, that we have, preserved to us, at least one relic of this first pastorate, one symbol (perhaps it may be called) of the unity of the successive generations of Christian believers here.

This sacramental cup, marked "C. C." (Chebacco Church), "1712," was in use six years in the first meeting-house; it was taken in the hands of Mr. Wise at every communion service for thirteen years; it was passed to the communicants by Deacons Goodhue and Story and Choate; in remembrance of their divine Lord it was pressed many times to the lips of some of the orignal members, who on this day in August, 1683, took upon them the covenant vows of this church, and, during the two hundred years that have now terminated, has been in constant use.

May this chalice be sacredly treasured in the future and aid in ministering to the spiritual life of an ever increasing company, in this goodly fellowship from century to century, until the Kingdom of God shall fully come.

II. The second period of special interest in the religious history of Chebacco includes the division of the church near the close of the ministry of the immediate successor of Mr. Wise, Rev. Theophilus Pickering, and the formation of a new one in 1746, with the settlement of its minister, Rev. John Cleaveland in 1747; and the reunion of these two churches on the eve of the Revolution, through the influence of Mr. Cleaveland, whose pastorate over the united church continued until his death in 1799.

To see clearly why and how this new church came into being, we need to set before us the religious situation, and to glance at Mr. Pickering's life and character, as disclosed chiefly through traditions and manuscript-papers in possession of members of the Pickering family and his own printed letters.

The son of John and Sarah (Burrill) Pickering, he was born Sept. 28, 1700, in the house owned by his father, which was built in the year 1651 by John Pickering from England,— the house now standing on Broad St., Salem, which has always been in the possession of the Pickering family, is in perfect preservation, and still owned by members of the same family and name.

Theophilus was the elder of two sons; and his younger brother Timothy, was the father of Col. Timothy Pickering of the Revolution, Secretary of War and afterwards of State in Washington's second administration.

John Pickering, their father, was by occupation a farmer. He was one of the Selectmen of Salem, and a Representative to the General Court. Dying in 1722, his "decease" is recorded in Felt's *Annals of Salem*, as a "loss to the community."

Theophilus Pickering was educated at Harvard College, graduating there in 1719, in a class of twenty-three members, thirteen of whom became clergymen. He was an earnest student, from his early years. In the first years of his college life the works of Derham on "Physico-Theology" and "Astro-Theology" enlisted his strong interest, and thoughout his college course, he gave much care and thought to extracting and transcribing, from these and other works in his " Extracta Notabilia," whatever seemed to him most worthy of preservation. A duodecimo manuscript volume of two hundred pages, with from fifty to sixty lines on a page, in clear and minute handwriting, and with diagrams, also drawn by him,—the whole copied from works that were published during his college life,—is still preserved in the family, and bears witness to his patient industry, as well as to his interest in the subject.

He possessed a taste also for the classical languages, with a familiarity and readiness in the use of Latin, and skill in the use of language in general. His scholarly tastes are well illustrated by the fact of his collecting a valuable library, many of the choicest volumes of which are still preserved.

After graduation Mr. Pickering taught school in Bridgewater for a year and a half; and in 1721 he preached regularly for some months in that town. In January, 1722, a committee of the General Court engaged him to preach as a missionary at Tiverton on Narragansett Bay, and he was employed in that work for nearly a year and a half.

See Appendix B.

During the last sickness of Rev. Mr. Wise, in April 1725, Mr. Pickering was invited by this parish to supply the pulpit four Sabbaths and continued preaching here through the spring and summer. Receiving then a call to the pastorate he accepted it and was ordained in the second meeting-house, October 13, 1725. The next year he built the house now occupied by Mr. Edwin Hobbs and made it his home the rest of his life, boarding, as his note-book states, in the family of Capt. Jonathan Cogswell from March 31, 1725 to June 16, 1736 and after that in his own house. He was never married.

Mr. Pickering was remarkable for his physical strength and muscular activity. He was noted also for his mechanical genius. As a skilful artificer in wood and in metal at the forge, he made some household articles for his own use, which have descended in the family. And the combined study-table and desk of his own invention and make, which served for his sermon-writing and his books of reference, is still in use in the house in which he was born. In keeping his financial accounts he was scrupulous and exact, and a high sense of honor guided all his business relations with others.

For about seventeen of the twenty-two years of his ministry Mr. Pickering seems to have given entire satisfaction to his people and to have been influential with them. In 1734 the parish voted that "in consideration of their love and affection to the Rev. Theophilus Pickering, they do freely, fully and absolutely convey to him all their right, title and interest in the land enclosed by the fence around his house and the well dug by him on the southeasterly side of the road." On account of the depreciation of the currency, they also added at this time fifty pounds to his salary and continued to increase it from time to time for the same reason, until it amounted to £232 per annum. Of his faithfulness and earnestness as a minister of the gospel we find evidence in the addition to the church during his pastorate, of about two hundred members, nearly as many as during that of Mr. Wise, though it was only half as long; and in the occurrence of at least one extensive revival of religion, the first in the history of this church, as the fruit of which seventy-six persons made a profession of religion.

The published testimony of his church after his death, respecting him, was: "We at Chebacco have (as we verily believe) had among us a man of God, a learned, orthodox, prudent and faithful minister of Jesus Christ, though not without failings, even as others; one whom we heard teaching and preaching the Gospel with pleasure, and we hope with profit; and whose memory will we trust be ever dear to us."

Of the preaching of the Rev. Mr. Whitefield, during his first tour through New England, in 1740, and of the remarkable religious revival which followed it, which has been usually called "The Great Awakening," Mr. Pickering was no uninterested observer.

When the renowned Evangelist, on this excursion eastward, on which he set out from Boston, Sept. 29th of that year, preached at Ipswich, on the hill in front of the first Congregational meeting-house, to some thousands, Mr. Pickering, as he tells us in one of his letters, was one of the many who went up from Chebacco and listened to his surpassing eloquence. This was the occasion of which Mr. Whitefield wrote: "The Lord gave me freedom, and there was a great melting in the Congregation." On his return from the east, he also preached at Ipswich, Oct. 4th.

Soon after, or at least early in the next year, the religious interest began to manifest itself in this community. Of a full account of it written in 1747, a part is as follows:

In the year 1741 and onwards it pleased God, out of his rich, free, and sovereign grace to bring upon the minds of many in this parish a deep concern about their future state and what they should do to be saved; and although something of this concern then spread itself over the land and in some places was very remarkable, we believe it was in none more so than in this place. The face of things was now changed; and engagedness to hear the word preached, christian conferences, private meetings for religious worship and assistance to each other in the way of life were what the minds of many appeared to be deeply concerned in, and engrossed much of our time. And we have undoubted grounds to conclude that at this time the free grace of God was richly displayed in the saving conversion of many among us."

With the progress of this religious work, which so deeply stirred the people of New England, there was soon developed among the churches and ministers everywhere a widening divergence of views with respect to the doctrinal preaching of the professional evangelists, the reality of certain inward experiences of which they made great account, the measures and methods they employed and the propriety of the degree of independence of church and ministerial authority maintained by them and their adherents.

The author of the work entitled *The Great Awakening*, published in 1842, remarks:

"The whole land, between 1742 and 1745 was full of angry controversy. Pastors were divided against pastors, churches against churches, and the members of the same church against each other, and against their pastor. The established rules of ecclesiastical order were set at defiance and openly trampled upon in the name of God. Ignorant and headstrong men were roaming at large, pretending to be under the immediate guidance of the Holy Ghost and slandering the best men in the land, and multitudes believed them. Religious meetings were often attended with disorder, from which the most reckless 'new measure' men of the nineteenth century would shrink back in absolute dismay. It is no wonder that good, judicious, sober men were alarmed, that they thought the conversion of some hundreds or thousands had been purchased at too dear a rate; and that they pronounced the revival a source of more evil than good."

So much this author concedes. And it was certainly the fact that early in 1743 there had come to be a division of the churches and ministers of our order into two great parties, which might be termed the right and left centre of the ecclesiastical host, the *right centre* believing in and zealously promoting the revival, acknowledging the existence of errors and disorders accompanying it, but condemning and contending against them and discerning abounding good which infinitely outweighed the attendant evils,—their extreme right wing, however, consisting of fanatics, rash and erratic Separatists, and disorganizers; the *left centre* (including some most excellent and pious clergymen), recognizing the reality of the revival and some good in it, but cautious or fearful about endorsing it as a whole, chiefly impressed by the errors, the disorders, the irrational excitements and the fanaticism accompanying or following it,— their extreme left wing composed of formalists, ultra-conservatives, those who were extremely high-church as regarded ecclesiastical authority, and rationalists.

While Mr. Pickering, who was distinguished for the moderation and coolness of his temper and the steadiness of his conduct, must perhaps be located in the left centre, he was certainly very near the dividing line. His piety and the evangelical character of his preaching were strongly endorsed by a large council in 1746, of which the Rev. Messrs. White of Gloucester and Wigglesworth of Hamilton were members, both of whom signed the famous *Boston Testimony* of ministers, in 1743, in favor of the revival. Mr. Pickering's own language also furnishes evidence of the correctness of his views on certain important points. In one of his letters published in 1742, he says:

"I don't ask you whether the conversion of a sinner be the work of God; this is undoubted. Or, whether the work of conversion be the same in the nature of it in every age; this is indisputable. Or, whether conviction precedes or accompanies conversion, and both may be called the work of God, that is, of his grace: this is admitted. Or, whether the work of conviction and conversion be now carried on in the land: this is conceded."

That Mr. Pickering not only discerned the spiritual reality of the revival, but also felt a genuine interest in it, he himself maintained in his letters, and there is no reason to doubt his sincerity. In another of these letters in 1742 he says:

"That numbers have been lately awakened to a careful inquiry into their spiritual state, and many convinced of their sin and danger and stirred up to duty, in a deep concern for their eternal salvation is what I am so far from disbelieving, that I am free to acknowledge it to the glory of God; and the rather because I doubt not but Divine Providence will shortly make it manifest, that what good has been done by some unprecedented measures is especially owing to the preventing mercy of God, in counter-working the devil in his subtle devices to undermine the churches of Christ."

Yet the errors and disorders which followed in the wake of the revival seemed to him so pernicious, that he shrank from actively participating in it.

One of the prevalent notions, apparently taught and cultivated by the revivalists, he refers to, in a letter of the same year, as:

"The conceit of some that the sudden starts of their fancy are immediate impressions from the Holy Spirit; that an impatient and furious desire to bear down all before them is a right zeal for the glory of God; and that they alone are the true ministers of Jesus Christ. Doubtless there are snares on either hand; and the Rev. Mr. Whitefield's concessions in his answer to the Bishop of London are matter of sober reflection, viz., that: 'Luke-warmness and zeal are the two rocks against which even well-meaning people are in danger of splitting — the bane of Christianity, and all ought to be thankful to that pilot who will teach them to steer a safe and middle course.'" "But," Mr. Pickering adds, "What if the pilot should mistake the vane for the compass?"

To Mr. Whitefield he wrote in 1745:

"I suppose you can't be ignorant of the schisms, variance, emulations, strife, railings and evil surmisings, things very different from the fruits of the Spirit, that have been increasing in more than four years ago. It is my real sentiment according to the best judgment I can form, that you are, at least, some unhappy occasion of our troubles."

In his own study of the measures of the revivalists, Mr. Pickering had observed some things, which he thought not scriptural and indicative of an effort to secure apparent results by an artificial excitement of natural feeling.

In a letter to Rev. Mr. Rogers of Ipswich, of Feb. 15, 1742, he writes: "You believe the Holy Spirit has of late remarkably descended upon many places. Would to God it might be according to your belief. But I am somewhat afraid that you have too great a dependence upon the remarkable effects or occurrences so often seen in your night meetings, at two of which I was present, on the 7th and 8th of January last."

Another thing that troubled Mr. Pickering was the disposition of the revivalists to cut loose from the teachings and guidance of the educated ministry, to weaken their authority and influence and to break down the regularly constituted organizations and arrangements for the maintenance of religion.

His exhortation in still another letter is:

"I desire you to be careful not to lead men into such a notion of the community of ministers, as may tempt them to slight the authority and administrations of their own pastors; but when you see people running mad after Paul and Apollos, and Cephas, rather say: Are ye not carnal? Moreover let not the deceiver beguile you into a belief of the necessity of destroying the form of religion because many professors may seem to deny the power. And I beseech you be cautious that while you endeavor reformation, your measures may not be subversive of our religious interests which were so dear to our forefathers. And therefore, I wish you to be of no council or aid to any party that may plot against our ministry, churches and colleges. What will not some men do? I pray God their machinations may be short-lived, and removed as a shepard's tent."

On the day when it was expected that a minister would be ordained over the Separatist Society, he writes:

"I went and stood before the chief house of entertainment where were many people and desiring them to attend, made a declaration in the following words. * * * * * 'Therefore I solemnly testify that such a procedure' (as this attempted ordination) 'is encouraging of unwarrantable separations, a disparaging of Ecclesiastical councils, a breach upon the fellowship of the churches, destructive of their peace and order, and highly injurious to the second church in Ipswich.' I then drew off and went to the Meeting-house where were many people without as well as within, and asking in those that were abroad I performed divine service; and at the close of the lecture I acquainted the assembly with the contents of the foregoing declaration, dismissed the people and went home."

Mr. Pickering was also sorely tried during these years (1742–45) by the efforts of certain ministers and exhorters

to preach in his parish without his invitation or consent, and
by the uncharitable way in which they alluded to him in
their prayers and their preaching. Against this treatment he
remonstrates in his letters to the Messrs. Rogers and to Mr.
Davenport (who was then at Ipswich) and in one of a little
later date to Mr. Whitefield, in a frank and decided manner,
yet with dignity and christian courtesy.

July 16, he writes:

"Instead of giving me better light and satisfaction by any reply to my
inquiry that you would dissolve my doubts as to certain views you hold)
you and your brother without advising with me, or first obtaining my consent, came last March into my parish and held several meetings in the
house for public worship; and have moreover been pleased to pray for me
in your assemblies, that God would open my eyes and that the scales might
fall from them; yea one of you thought fit, publicly, in the hearing of my
people, to call me their blind minister."

This attitude of Mr. Pickering towards the revival movement and the measures adopted to promote it and the character of his preaching occasioned, on the part of those among
his people who were in the fullest sympathy with the work, a
growing dissatisfaction with him throughout the year 1743;
which led them finally to present to him, March 12, 1744, a
statement in writing of certain grievances or "occasions of
disquietude" (as they styled them) signed by twenty-six of
the sixty-three members of his church, with the intimation
that they should withdraw from his preaching, unless the
causes of this disquietude were removed.

These grievances in reality charged him with not preaching
plainly the distinctive doctrines of the Bible, with a want of
interest in his ministerial work, with worldliness of spirit and
conduct and with opposition to the work of grace going on
among them.

Mr. Pickering's indignation at these charges, as well as his
determination to prevent as far as possible any departure from
the established usages of the church, carried him to an extreme in the exercise of his authority as church moderator

towards the disaffected brethren and in his personal treatment of them, which only served to widen the breach between him and them, and to confirm them in their purpose of secession from the church.

On the 13th of January, 1746, at the house of Daniel Giddinge, sixteen members of the church resolved to form a society, that they might have the gospel of Christ preached to them; on the 15th they went up to the meeting-house where there was then a church meeting, and "declared to Mr. Pickering and the church publicly that they had separated themselves from them;" and on the 20th they completed the formation of a "Separate Society," thirty-eight men entering into "a solemn covenant and league to set up the worship of God agreeably to his word revealed in the Scriptures." Of this body Capt. Robert Choate was moderator and William Giddinge clerk.

Notwithstanding this decisive action the church called a council of nine churches, May 20, to consider the whole matter; of which Rev. John White, of the First church, Gloucester, a son-in-law of Rev. Mr. Wise, and warmly interested in the revival, was the moderator.

Although the disaffected brethren declined the proposal of this council to join in calling a mutual council, they yet, at its invitation, presented all their articles of complaint and the evidence to sustain them, to the members of the council as private christians.

With all the facts thus before them the majority of the council in their result, June 10th, after a thorough investigation, judged that there was no ground for the charge of a want of interest on the part of Mr. Pickering in his ministerial work, or of a neglect of pastoral visits; that there was no reason for doubting his piety, for believing that he had been worldly in spirit, or had conducted improperly in business affairs; and they endorsed fully the evangelical character of his preaching. On the other hand they were of the opinion that he had been negligent about examining candidates for admission to the church respecting their religious experiences, that he had failed to examine early and thoroughly into the nature of the religious experiences among his flock, as he ought to have done; and that his treatment of the aggrieved at first had given them just ground of offence, but that he had offered them such satisfaction that they ought to forgive him. The council, therefore, regarded the withdrawal as unjustifiable and reproachful to religion, and the action of the disaffected, in setting up a separate assembly for worship, as contrary to the known order of the churches.

A minority of six — including three ministers — dissented, considering that the disaffected persons had real grounds of grievance with their pastor, which still remained, and that the withdrawal was not reproachful to religion nor deserving of the censure of the church. Yet even they did not justify the withdrawal in all the circumstances of it, and they exhorted both parties to put away what had been "unchristian-like" in spirit and behavior, and carefully endeavor a reunion.

Whether this protracted struggle, involving the alienation of friends and causing continual anxiety, disappointment and depression to Mr. Pickering on account of this dismembering of the church and parish, unfavorably affected his health or not, we do not know; but in a little more than a year, after a very short sickness he died of a fever, Oct. 7, 1747 — closing his ministry of twenty-two years at the early age of forty-seven; and his remains lie in the old grave yard.

In the *Boston Gazette or Weekly Journal* of Tuesday, Nov. 10, 1747, appeared the following notice:

"Chebacco in Ipswich, Oct. 11, 1747. On Monday last died here of a fever and this day was interred the Rev. Theophilus Pickering, in the forty-seventh year of his age; and after he had been Pastor of the Second Church in Ipswich 22 years. He had been as generally esteemed and loved by his people, perhaps, as most of his Order, until some of the last years of his life; when unhappy Alienations on Account of his Doctrine and Conduct, discovered themselves in many of his Flock, who brought Accusation against him relating hereto before the Church and at length before a Council of the neighboring Churches Convened for that Purpose, who judged the Alienation and Disaffection to be without Sufficient Ground. Under the pressure of so great Trouble, as he was Exercised with, he was Observed to bear up with Uncommon Evenness and Patience of Mind, and dy'd at last in a desirable Tranquility of Soul as to Spiritual Concerns: Preaching the Doctrines of Grace by a free Profession that he was a sinful Creature, who had nothing of his own to recommend him to God: that his alone Expectation was from the imputed Righteousness of the Redeemer, and that he had a Comfortable Hope of Acceptance through that Righteousness."

The church nothing daunted by his loss, loyal to his memory and still maintaining the justice of their cause, prepared and adopted Dec. 31, 1747, and published early the next year: "A Letter from Second church in Ipswich to their separated brethren in defence of their deceased pastor and themselves, against the injurious charges of the said separated brethren in a late print of theirs, by giving a more just and true account of the things that preceded the separation."

Instead also of entertaining a proposal made by the seceders, Jan. 14, 1748, for a conference to consider the possibility of a union of the two bodies, they immediately declined it, and called a council of six churches from Boston, Cambridge Reading and Salem to pass judgment on the procedure of the withdrawing members; which body after two sessions on the 19th and 30th of July, 1748, gave decision that the new Separate organization was not a Congregational church, and exhorted the brethren composing it to be reconciled to the church they had left.

On the 3d of January, 1749, Mr. Nehemiah Porter, a native of Hamilton and a graduate of Harvard College in 1745, who had already supplied the pulpit for some time, was ordained the third pastor of the old church. Of his ministry here of seventeen years very little is known. Near its close a disagreement arose between him and some of his church; and the mutual council, called to consider the matter, advised him to "take blame to himself and to give the aggrieved brethren such satisfaction as they had a right to demand." This he refused to do, and, as a majority of the church sustained him, the disaffected, considering that there had been a breach of the covenant on the part of said majority in so doing, withdrew and were received into communion with the new church.

A difficulty afterwards respecting his salary occasioned other councils and finally the dissolving of the relation between him and his church and parish, by a decision of referees, in June 1766.

Mr. Porter removed to Yarmouth, Nova Scotia, where there was a Chebacco colony; and, after founding a Congregational church there and preaching to it several years, returned to his native state and was the pastor of a church in Ashfield, Franklin Co., from Dec. 21, 1774 until his death Feb. 20, 1820, when he lacked but a month of a hundred years in age. His active service in the ministry did not end until he was in his eighty-eight year, and he continued to preach occasionally for a long time afterward, sometimes exhorting and praying in public up to the last year of his life.

The testimony of one of his contemporaries was, that "as a preacher he sustained a very respectable character; if not a star of the first magnitude, yet shining with a clearness and degree of lustre, which rendered him an ornament to the church. The doctrines he firmly believed were such as are emphatically called the doctrines of grace; and these he inculcated in all his sermons, which were instructive, impressive and delivered with force and fervor." His ministerial labors were attended with success in large additions to his church.

One or two anecdotes told of him may help to illustrate his character. He was a chaplain in the American army, at the surrender of Burgoyne, and used to say with a great deal of animation, "I conquered him. The decisive blow was struck, and the battle decided while I was holding a season of special prayer, in a retired place, with a few pious soldiers." Mr.

Porter had great firmness and decision of character. Once, when preaching on politics, a gentleman of the opposite party arose in his pew and said, "Mr. Porter, you had better let that subject alone." Upon which, with a stamp of the foot and great energy, he exclaimed, "Silence!" and proceeded with his discourse.

On his grave stone, near the Congregational church in Ashfield, is the following epitaph: "Mr. Porter was a faithful minister of Christ: with long life he was satisfied: he fell asleep in Jesus in hope of a joyful resurrection and a blessed immortality. 'The righteous shall be in everlasting remembrance.'"

THE NEW CHURCH AND ITS FOUNDERS.

Turning now from the fortunes of the old church, to the branch, which had been sundered from it, had taken root so vigorously and become so thrifty, we find that the seceders — nine men and thirty-two women — were, by a council of two Separatist churches, from Boston and Plainfield, Conn., justified in the course they had taken, aided in preparing articles of faith and discipline and a covenant and organized as the fourth church in Ipswich, (that at Hamilton being the third), on the twenty-second of May 1746; and that on the seventeenth of December, this church elected Francis Choate and Daniel Giddinge, ruling Elders, and Eleazar Craft and Solomon Giddinge, deacons.

Its members and all who worshipped with them were, by law, obliged to pay a property tax to the old parish, (as that was a territorial organization), and therefore to carry a double financial burden; until, after six years of opposition to their

* The ruling Elders were officers provided for in the "Cambridge Platform," who, (with the pastor) should constitute a sort of "session," to do the business of the church and to carry out its direction. "This office never had the unanimous sanction of the churches and had become nearly obsolete before 1683." It was now, however, first established in this church but dropped out of use in less than fifty years.

application to the General Court, the petitioners, fifty-seven in number, obtained an act of incorporation, Dec. 8, 1752, and with their families and estates were made a distinct and separate precinct; and their house of worship—the *third* in Chebacco—was erected the same year.

Remembering that *this* also was entirely a laymen's movement to secure a more evangelical faith, a more vigorous spiritual life in the church and greater freedom in religious matters, whom do we find to be the leaders and energetic workers in it?

Of the new *parish* Joseph Perkins was one of the founders and prominent members, its clerk from the beginning for over twenty years and its treasurer for nearly the same length of time. For a long period he kept a tavern nearly opposite the church and died April 4, 1805, at the age of eighty-five.

Among others who were the moving spirits in this Separatist Religious Society, the office-bearers in the new *church*, not only by virtue of their position, but because they were actually foremost in its history for many years, its chief directors and upholders, are brought conspicuously before us, at the opening of its career.

One of them was Elder Francis Choate, a son of "Governor" Thomas Choate whose abilities and force of character had made him a leader in the affairs of the community and efficient in his devotion to the interests of the church in Mr. Wise's day and later and who lived to witness the scenes of the great revival, dying in 1745, at the age of seventy-four. Francis, born Sept. 13, 1701, was bred under Mr. Wise's preaching was a young man of twenty-four when Mr. Pickering began his ministry, was converted in the revival of 1727, and from that time onward was known as a man of firm principle, familiar with religious doctrines and of uncommon depth and fervor of piety. He was most heartily in sympathy with the wide spread and intense religious interest which Whitefield's preaching awakened and of which he gives an account in his journal. In the secession from the old church he was one of the chief actors and unsparingly devoted all his intellectual strength and energy to the promotion of the welfare and growth of the new one. The council which constituted that church met at his house, (now Mr. Lamont Burnham's, occupied by Mr. Frank Andrews); he was its first moderator; and on his grounds took place the ordination of its first minister, whose right-hand man and warm personal friend he was ever after.

For thirty years a Justice of the Peace and almost constantly employed in law business and in civil affairs as a town officer, acute and skilful in debate, Esq. Choate became the strong staff of the young church whose cause he espoused in the maturity of his manhood and retained the fervor of his attachment to it to the end of his life.

Another of these "New Lights" of Chebacco was Dea. Eleazer Craft, a son of Benjamin and Abigail (Harris) Craft, born in Roxbury, May 5, 1711. Through the influence of his brother Benjamin, who was also one of the Separatists, and was a Louisbourg soldier, Eleazar came to Chebacco, and married Aug. 25, 1738, Martha Low, who died Sept. 28, 1797, aged eighty-three. Dea. Craft was a farmer and lived not far from the corner of the old and new roads to Manchester. In the preparation, Sept. 15, 1747, of the "Plain Narrative of the proceedings, which caused a separation of a number of aggrieved brethren from the second church in Ipswich," he took an active part. Elected deacon at the formation of the church, he was, from Nov. 20, 1765, until his death, May 28, 1790, at the age of seventy-eight, a Ruling Elder and was the last one who held that office. A faithful church officer for forty-four years, he was very highly esteemed for his ardent piety and uniform christian deportment.

Still a fourth leader of the Separatists was Ensign James Eveleth, whose father Joseph moved to Chebacco in 1674 and was remarkable for his piety as well as for the great age to which he attained. His is the first name on the record of those who joined the Chebacco church after its organization in 1683. In a deed distributing some of his property by gift among members of his family, in 1719, the year after the building of the second meeting-house, he directs his children "to pay to ye church of Christ in Chebacco forty shillings, to be laid out and improved towards ye buying a piece of plate for ye use of said church."

A great granddaughter, (who was fifteen years old at his death), used to describe in her old age the visit made to him by Rev. Mr. Whitefield in 1740, her mind always retaining, as she said, a "vivid impression of the solemnity of the scene presented when Whitefield knelt upon the floor and received, from the lips that could relate a christian experience of nearly a hundred years, a truly patriarchal blessing." Living to witness the scenes of the great awakening, he died Dec. 1, 1745, at the age of one hundred and five years.

His oldest son, John, was the first Chebacco boy to receive a liberal education. A graduate of Harvard in 1689, he preached at Enfield and at Manchester for a short time, at Stowe, seventeen years, then at Kennebunkport and Biddeford Me., until 1729, and died at Kittery, Me., Aug. 1, 1734.

James, the youngest son of Joseph, received from his father in 1715 a deed of lands in Chebacco, the consideration being "that naturall law and parentall affection which I have and do bare unto my loveing son James Eveleth, of said Chebacco in Ipswich, as also for his dutifull carriage towards me, and his faithfull serving of me."

This son, Ensign James, was not only one of the twenty-six, who in 1744 presented to Mr. Pickering their "causes of disquietude," but was also one of the four who had come so directly into antagonism with the minister, as to feel obliged to send him, April 29, their statement of "additional grievances." He was also one of the nineteen who signed the "Plain Narrative" and was appointed one of a committee of two, to tender an invitation, Jan. 27, 1746, to Rev. John Cleaveland, then of Boston, to visit Chebacco and preach there. Mr. Eveleth was a farmer and lived at the Falls, where Mr. Luther Burnham's house now stands. Through his only son, James, descended Aaron Eveleth, a soldier in the Revolution, among whose children was the late Capt. Jonathan Eveleth.

That Elder Daniel Giddinge (a town-representative in 1758, who died Oct. 25, 1771, aged sixty-seven), was an efficient co-worker with Messrs. Perkins, Choate, Craft and Eveleth, there is good reason to believe. The first meeting to form the Separate Society was held at his house. And his vigilance and promptness to act for its interests, as well his ability to wield the pen with some pertinence and force, come out clearly in a brief document printed by him in Boston, Feb. 12, 1748, the opening of which explains the occasion and intent of it and is as follows:

"Whereas, the subscriber, one of the brethren that left the Rev. Mr. Pickering's church, being in Boston and perceiving that the 'Answer to the aggrieved brethren's Plain Narrative' is dispersed among the members of the General Assembly now sitting, containing among a number of groundless insinuations, a few things objected to some of the facts in said Narrative, tending to discredit the same and bring an odium on the narrators, dispersed as I suppose to prejudice the said Honorable Court against us at this time: To prevent this, I will say, as what I am ready to verify and make good, as follows:"

Then he proceeds to give what he calls a "brief statement in eight particulars;" which is clear, concise and to the point.

Further light is thrown upon the intellectual and religious character of these office-bearers and their associates, by two things which accompanied the organization of this new church and the settlement of its first minister.

The first was the preparation and adoption of an elaborate code of eighteen articles of faith and discipline.* How much

* See Appendix C.

their past ecclesiastical experiences had to do with suggesting the necessity of these articles and with putting them into the shape they assumed, may be inferred from the few paragraphs I will read from them.

"1st. That we will have such officers as Christ Jesus has appointed and ordained in his holy Word, viz.: a Pastor or Pastors, Ruling Elders and Deacons.

2d. That no person shall be admitted to either of said offices, unless he has Scripture qualifications evidently appearing, to the satisfaction of the church.

3d. That the Church shall have the sole power of electing and appointing all the officers of the Church.

5th. That no person shall be admitted as a member of said Church, but such as shall give a particular account of a saving work of the Spirit of God upon his or her soul, to the satisfaction of the Church.

7th. That we will not admit of any person to minister to us in holy things who shall refuse to submit to an examination of the state of his soul by such a number of the brethren as the Church from time to time shall think fit to appoint; and shall give to them a declaratory account of a work of grace wro't upon his soul; who shall also sign these articles before he shall be ordained to the Pastoral care of this Church.

13th. That neither Pastor nor Elders shall invite any person to preach, until they are satisfyed that he has a work of grace wro't on his soul.

14th. We believe that all the gifts and graces that are bestowed on any of the members are to be improved for the good of the whole; in order to which there ought to be such a gospel freedom, whereby the Church may know where every particular gift is, that it may be improved in its proper place, and to its right end, for the glory of God, and for the good of the Church.

15th. The confession of faith agreed upon by the Assembly of Divines at Westminster we fully agree to in every respect, as to the substance of the same.

16th. We would always have recourse to the Platform agreed upon by the Synod at Cambridge in New England, A.D. 1649, and for the further explanation of our own sentiments respecting church discipline, etc., we will always be willing to be guided thereby with the following exceptions and emendations:

Chap. 10, Section 6. Respecting the Direction of a Council being necessary in order for a Church to remove their Pastor we do except against.

Sec. 8. We judge the Elders ought to call the Church together when desired by any one member; and whenever the Church is mett, the brethren have a right, one by one, asking leave to declare their mind without interruption or hindrance, and that the Elders have no power to adjourn or dissolve meetings without a vote of the Church.

Chap. 13. *Sec.* 4. Respecting magistrates having a power to force people to contribute for the support of the gospel, we except against, being not intrusted with the support of the same; that the Church have power to deal with all such as will not, if able, contribute to the support of the gospel, we hold, and also that by the Holy Scriptures Gifts may be received, but not forced from any without.

Chap. 17. *Sec.* 9. Respecting the magistrates having a coercial power, or right to punish a church that rends itself off from the churches, being by them judged incorrigible and schismatick, we except against.

18th. Lastly, That if notwithstanding our great care in the admition of a Pastor or Pastors, or other officers, any or either of them should deny or walk contrary to these Doctrines, and persist therein, then in such a case said person or persons shall no longer have any power or authority in the Church, but shall be, and hereby are, debarred therefrom, until manifest tokens of their Humiliation and Repentance."

If these articles are not Calvinistic, Low-church, Independent, Democratic, then to what could you apply these epithets? There is certainly no room in them for clerical authority, or a dead formalism to lurk; nor could one charge this church with any lack of self-control. These sentences recall and illustrate Mr. Wise's declaration that "democracy is Christ's government in church and state."

The other thing particularly noticeable is the cool, business-like way in which these laymen proceeded to execute the provisions of these articles in their selection of a minister and to sit in judgment on the theological and spiritual qualifications of a candidate for the pastoral office before giving him a call to settle with them. Their record reads as follows:

"Dec. 17, 1746. At a meeting of the newly-gathered Congregational Church of Christ in Chebacco, upon adjournment, it was voted: That John Cleaveland be desired to declare his principles, which he did as follows:"

Then is given what is entitled "The Principles and Fundamentals of Mr. John Cleaveland's Faith," in twenty articles, an elaborate and minute creed, essentially that of the Westminster Assembly of Divines, but wrought into shape by his own thought and expressed, in the main, in his own language, and closing with these words:

"These articles I .... to believe, not only speculatively and scientifically, but also .... and practically through rich grace and boundless and matchless .... in the dear Redeemer." "John Cleaveland."*

The Record continues:

"These .... had a good and unanimous acceptance by the .... That Mr. John Cleaveland should be pastor of this church; .... our choice of Mr. John .... for pastor be laid before the society for their concurrence; That a .... tee be chosen to give the said Mr. Cleaveland a call to the pastoral ......"

Where could you find a company of men more competent to manage their ecclesiastical affairs than that one? Surely there was no need in Chebacco, an hundred and thirty-seven years ago, of a Presbytery or a Bishop to tell these intelligent, reflecting Bible-students, spiritually enlightened, what to believe, or who was a suitable religious teacher and guide for them. These godly, liberty-loving but self-controlled, Protestant, Americanized Englishmen of the fourth generation, had not let go their English Bible as the Inspired Word, nor sold their God-given birthright for any mess of pottage, whether prelatical or presbyterial on the one hand, or rationalistic or "theistic" on the other.

In these Christian laymen is brilliantly displayed the sturdy Puritan character of the seventeenth century ennobled by the "Great Awakening" of the eighteenth century.

REV. JOHN CLEAVELAND.

But who was this John Cleaveland and what were his antecedents that he should so exactly suit this new Chebacco Church? His great grandfather, Moses Cleaveland was a first settler in this country, from that same old Ipswich, England, from which had come some of the founders of *our* Ipswich. His grandfather, Josiah Cleaveland, removed from Chelmsford, Mass., to the fertile meadows of the Quinebaug in Can-

---

* See Appendix D.

terbury, the central southern town of Windham County, in the northeast corner of Connecticut, in 1693, being one of its original settlers. His father Josiah Cleaveland was one of the most influential men in his day in all town matters there. Throughout his life a pillar in the Congregational church, he left it, at his death, in 1751, his part of the ownership of the meeting-house and £200 in money.

Very early in the history of the Great Awakening, a deep religious thoughtfulness spread through Canterbury. "Many leading members of the church and among them Josiah Cleaveland were aroused to new interest, and became active in promoting the work." Among the children and youth, hopefully converted, was his son John, the seventh of eleven children, born April 11, 1722, who united with the church in 1740.

From a fragment of an autobiography and diary, we learn that John's early life was spent upon the farm, with the three winter months at school, and amid the influences of a christian home. An injury caused by an ambitious attempt to outstrip others in stone-wall building disabled him for severe physical labor and, beginning preparation for College in September, 1739, he entered Yale in 1741, in a class which graduated twenty-seven members.

Of his College course he writes:

"I took special delight in the study of the Greek Testament, Logic, Natural Philosophy and History. But in the midst of all these studies I found the Gospel to be that which my soul was then most captivated with, not merely the doctrinal part, which however was divinely sweet, but the practical and vital part, it being the time of my first love, when the candle of the Lord shined with divine lustre and efficacious splendor on my soul."

During the first winter in College he hears "heavenly news from Canterbury;" his brother Ebenezer and his sisters are converted; his father's house has become a little Bethel. His journal in the spring vacation gives a glimpse of the progress of the revival in his native place and indicates great religious interest and activity there.

Just at that time, however, (May, 1742) the government of Connecticut, acting on the opinion of the General Consociation of churches that "the growing extravagances and excesses accompanying the religious excitement throughout the state were to be attributed to the intrusion of unauthorized itinerants and the holding of free religious conferences," passed an act to correct and prevent these evils by forbidding the preaching of evangelists and exhorters and the speaking in meeting by laymen, without permission from constituted authority. This extraordinary law, of course, excited great opposition and only aggravated the disorders it was intended to cure, and not more in other places than in Canterbury where in 1744 the religious disturbances had greatly increased.

The parish (and a minority of the church) had determined to settle a minister to whom a large majority of the church— earnest supporters of the revival movement—were opposed. The latter had therefore withdrawn from the meeting-house, and were holding religious services in private houses, conducted by laymen. John Cleaveland and his brother Ebenezer, in the summer vacation of that year, being members of the church, of course attended with them.

The church and state authorities took the ground that every church in the state was subject to the "Saybrook Platform," except by formal dissent at the time of its organization, and that no subsequent vote by any number of its members could change its status; that the minority at Canterbury were therefore the church; and that the majority by declaring themselves Congregational according to the Cambridge platform, (as they had done in 1743, after carefully investigating the origin and history of their church, through a committee), had forfeited their ecclesiastical standing and legal privileges and were a body of "Separatists" whose meetings were unlawful.

On the return of the Cleavelands to College, in November, they were summoned before President Clap, on the charge of violating a law of the College which also forbade attendance on "Separate" meetings. They argued their case with force; but although they pleaded for delay, a bill was immediately issued against them, suspending them from all the rights and privileges of the College, for violating the law of God, the Colony and the College, until satisfaction should be made in the form of a public confession to this effect. This they could not, in conscience, do. They sent to the Faculty a very respectful and humble petition to be restored to college standing, but instead of accepting it, the government of the College administered a formal admonition, Nov. 19.* Their collision with the authorities was very widely published and excited great sympathy. Their mother and other friends sent them letters, entreating them to be true to their own convictions, and not to deny their church and wrong God and their own consciences by making a false confession. As they did thus hold fast to the position they had taken, President Clap summoned them to the Hall, sometime in the month of December and announced the formal sentence of expulsion.

The next May the brothers sent in a memorial to the Legislature of the state, praying for a redress of their grievances and to be immediately restored to their standing in College.

"In a well written document they recite the reasons for their father's separating, with a majority of the church members, from the religious society in Canterbury; and complain that they have been punished for that which was not against College law. They say near the close of their petition, and with reason, as people now think: 'May it please your Honors, as we understand the laws of this colony, the Congregational persuation is as much under the countenance of the laws of this colony as the Saybrook Platformists are; and therefore we think it hard measure indeed to be cut off from our College privileges, merely for being of the Congregational persuation, and acting agreeable thereto, while the Saybrook Platformists, professors of the Church of England, Seven-day and other Baptists and Quakers have and have had free liberty to enjoy all the privileges of College, their principles and practices in the vacancies of College agreeable thereto notwithstanding.'"†

*See Appendix E.
†Pres. Woolsey's Historical Address.

Their petition, however, was dismissed without action of either house.

At a later day, as Mr. Cleaveland himself writes: "Through the application to the College Corporation of a number of ministers in the neighborhood of Chebacco, accompanied with reflections made by me to the Reverend President, which were 'satisfactory', a diploma of A. M., and my standing in my class, (that of 1745), were granted me in 1763. The honorary degree of A. M. was also conferred upon him in 1782 by Dartmouth College.

For several months of the year 1745 Mr. Cleaveland studied theology with Rev. Philemon Robbins of Branford, Conn., an able and popular preacher and a warm advocate of the revival measures. In August he began preaching in some of the "new light" churches of Windham county, and was desired by the one in his native town to become its minister. The next month he was invited to a "Separate" church in Boston, then worshipping in the old Huguenot meeting-house in School street; and he supplied their pulpit about eight or ten months. Nov. 12th, he wrote to Mr. Robbins, his instructor, that he had preached sixty times in and around Boston, and that the Lord had been with him in a wonderful manner.

In response to an invitation of Jan. 27, 1746, from James Eveleth and Francis Choate, as he writes in his journal: "Feb. 17th, I rode to Chebacco and preached in the meeting-house, each of the four days following. When I took my leave of them, the assembly was watered with tears."

On the 20th of May he was the moderator of the Council which organized the new church in this village and preached here again in August. A formal request in the autumn from the Boston society to become their pastor he was still holding under consideration, when the Chebacco church made their overtures to him in December.

It seems natural to suppose that it was the somewhat similar experience of trial and conflict through which his own church in Canterbury had passed and the additional troubles he had suffered in College, for conscience sake, during precisely the same years, as well as his intense interest in the revival moment and the complete harmony of his views with those of the new church in Chebacco, that drew him into an especially close sympathy with them, when he was balancing between the two places and decided him to cast in his lot with the people here as their fellow prisoner in the bonds of the gospel.

Having accepted their call Dec. 26, he was ordained Feb. 25, 1747, in the presence of a large audience, though the service was held in the open air, at an inclement season.

One of his grandsons (not a clergyman), in a foot-note to the printed pages of his journal, has, I grieve to say, viewed this matter of his settlement here from altogether another standpoint, and suggested an additional if not an entirely different motive for his decision, as follows:

"From a social and worldly point of view the Boston invitation must have been far more attractive than the Chebacco call. But he had found in that plain community of farmers and fishermen, one magnet of superior power. I have no doubt that it was the bright and comely Mary Choate Dodge,— mentioned later in his journal as his 'dear and loving spouse'— who *virtually* determined the question where he should stay."

We ought not for an instant to admit this soft impeachment; and yet the very next recorded event in his life was his marriage, on the fifteenth of July following, to Mary, the only daughter of Mr. Parker Dodge of Hamilton.

From the year 1749, Mr. and Mrs. Cleaveland lived on Spring street, in a house whose site is now occupied by that of Mrs. David Choate; and it was in that mansion that they entertained the renowned Whitefield as their guest in the autumn of 1754. The entry in Mr. Cleaveland's journal is:

"Oct. 28. Rev. George Whitefield came to our house and preached the next morning in our meeting-house. He then went to Cape Ann, preached twice, and came and lodged with us that night. I think it a great honor to have his company."

This is not the place to attempt to delineate the character of Mr. Cleaveland or to give a sketch of the ministry of this zealous man of God, this eloquent preacher and indefatigable worker. But some brief mention of three passages in his life may be appropriate, to illustrate the kind and quality of his labors and services for this church and parish.

1. The first of these takes us on to the years 1760–64. The country had just passed through the long and exciting French war which had absorbed the public mind. Many had returned from army and camp life, demoralized in their principles and habits; there was a great increase of Sabbath desecration and profanity, and even in the churches it was a time of religious declension.

At this aspect of things, on return from a temporary absence, Mr. Cleaveland's spirit was stirred within him. With his strong faith in the Bible doctrine of prayer, he persuaded his church to agree to spend one day every quarter of the year "in a congregational fasting and praying," as he says, "for the outpouring of God's spirit upon all nations agreeable to the concert for prayer, first entered into in Scotland, some years since (in 1744); and also to spend a part of a day once a fortnight in a private religious conference. This for near half a year was held once a week, for the most part, and divers at those meetings were favored with a remarkable spirit of prayer for the rising generation".

From this significant statement we learn the origin of the *Quarterly Fast*, in which three of the other churches in Ipswich began to unite in 1780, and which was maintained here for a hundred years and more—the centennial year of its establishment being observed by an exceedingly interesting service in our meeting-house, Dec. 31, 1860.

This record also discloses the earliest observance, in this community, of the Monthly concert of prayer for the conversion of the world, for which a circular invitation was sent out from Scotland in 1746, five hundred copies of which were sent to New England. How enlightened and comprehensive Mr. Cleaveland's views were upon this subject of the responsibility of the church for the spiritual welfare of the whole world, and how dear this object was to his heart, appears also from the following remarkable letter which he wrote in 1763, on the duty of undertaking the christianizing of the American Indians:

"Very Dear Sir: Since I have understood that the preliminary articles of Peace are ratified, by which the vast country on the eastern side of the river Mississippi, from the source of said river to the ocean, is ceded" (i.e. by France) "to his Brittanic majesty, I have been ready to think we never had so loud a call and so wide a door opened, to use endeavors to propagate the gospel and spread the savour of the knowledge of Christ among the Indian tribes, which inhabit or rather range in the extended wilds of North America, as now we have. A view to christianize the Heathen was a pious motive with our Forefathers to come into this America at first; and what all along has been an obstruction to their conversion God has now removed. And as God has now given the English nation all North America, it can't be thought that we render again according to the benefit done unto us, if we neglect to improve all proper means to communicate to the heathen the inestimable treasure of the Gospel, which God has long indulged us with and now secured the enjoyment of to us, against those that ever have sought to deprive us of the same. Moreover, can it be supposed that God has wonderfully crowned the British arms with success and given us all this vast country which is now ceded to us, merely for Great Britain's and British American Colonies' sake — seeing the promise is of the heathen to Christ for an inheritance?"

Surely Mr. Cleaveland and his church were fully abreast of the times in which they lived. Within three years of the time of entering upon the use of these most scriptural means for securing a spiritual reformation there followed a religious revival, which, engrossed the attention of the whole community and for the intensity of feeling experienced by those who were the subjects of it and the number of them — in all about an hundred persons, — as well as for the spread of it into many other places round about, has never been paralleled, in the history of this church.

Mr. Cleaveland's published account of this, in 1767 — in a

pamphlet of some thirty-two pages, entitled: "A short and plain narrative of the late work of God's spirit in Chebacco in Ipswich in the years 1763 and 1764"* — is a story of exceeding interest throughout.†

THE REUNION OF THE TWO CHURCHES AND PARISHES.

2. Another of Mr. Cleaveland's more important services was that which he performed in securing the reunion of the two churches here. Coming to Chebacco, as he did, when the controversy between the two alienated divisions of the original church and parish was at its height and fiercely raging, at the invitation of one of the two contending parties, he of course identified himself with its cause and became its champion. The last of the four pamphlets relative to this controversy, entitled: "*Chebacco narrative rescued from the charge of falsehood and partiality; by a friend of truth,*" was believed to have been written by him and gives some idea of his bold spirit in that contest and of his style as a writer.‡

The fact is therefore all the more noteworthy that he, the very man who had thus so hotly assailed the opposite camp, succeeded within a generation, in reconciling those brethren mutually offended and estranged for so long a time, — carrying on the process of uniting the fractured members and the healing, unto perfect soundness, so that apparently no trace of ill feeling remained.

Indeed the members of the *old* parish must have learned through their observation of him as a christian minister, their intercourse with him as a fellow townsman, and their knowledge of his kindness to the soldiers of their families in the

* See Appendix F.

† One of the Manchester converts was Edward Lee, a sailor, "who caught the flame of divine love from the glowing soul of the Chebacco minister and attended his preaching the rest of his life." Thirty years afterward Mr. Cleaveland preached the funeral sermon of this man at Manchester, in December, 1793; and a brief biographical sketch of him was published in 1849, by the American S. S. Union.

‡ See Appendix G.

French War, to respect and appreciate and love him, in order to make as they did—though still stronger financially than his parish—the first proposal for reunion, within three months after the dismission of their last minister, Mr. Porter, in 1766. The *first* real step towards this was the arrangement made in 1768, to worship together, half the year in each meeting-house; the *second* was the agreement, in 1770, that the old parish should pay four-sevenths of Mr. Cleaveland's salary; and the *decisive* step was (by proposal of the old *church*) a joint meeting of the two churches at the centre school-house, April, 1774, for a conference relative to a union, and the unanimous vote by each church, separately, "to bury forever, as a church, all former differences between them and the other church and to acknowledge the other a sister church in charity and fellowship."

By vote of each church at the same place, the first Monday in June, with a concurrence in their action by the two parishes, July 1, an ecclesiastical council, to assist and advise the two churches in uniting in one, was called, which met, Oct. 4th, in the new meeting-house. It consisted of the other four churches in Ipswich and the church in Byfield, and Rev. Mr. Leslie was its moderator.

To settle a difficulty of longstanding between the new church and that in Manchester, (occasioned by the former church's receiving to communion, members of the latter under discipline), there was an adjournment until the 25th. This obstacle having been removed, a plan of union, articles of faith and a covenant, the preparation of which had been assigned to a committee, were reported to the Council, accepted and recommended to the two churches. The churches, also, after deliberation, passed a unanimous vote of acceptance; and these documents were subscribed in the presence of the council by Dea. Seth Story, moderator, and five other brethren of the old church, and the pastor and twenty-two brethren of the new.

The Compact was in part, as follows:

"Heads of Agreement for uniting the Second and Fourth Churches of Ipswich into one Congregational Church, come into in the presence of a council of Churches."

"1. We, the Second and Fourth Churches of Ipswich, covenant and agree to become one Congregational church, under the name or style of the Second Church of Ipswich.

3. We covenant and agree to receive the word of God contained in the Scriptures of the Old and New Testament to be our absolute and only rule relative to the doctrines of faith, the worship of God, church-government and discipline, all relative duties, and a virtuous life and conversation.

4. As we aim to be a true *Protestant* Church in our united state, we covenant and agree to profess unity of faith with the Protestant church in general, by adopting that system of Christian doctrine held forth in the Westminster shorter catechism and the New England Confession of Faith; it being a sound, orthodox system or summary of Scripture doctrine, according to our understanding of the word of God.

5. And, as we aim to be a strictly *Congregational* Church in point of church-government and discipline in our united state, we covenant and agree to adhere to the platform of church government and discipline drawn up by a synod at Cambridge in New England, A. D. 1648, as containing our sentiments, in the general, relative to a church-state, its power, its officers, their ordination, the qualifications for church-membership, admission of members, the communion of churches, &c., &c., — in a word relative to church-government in general.

And now, as a visible political union among a number of visible saints is necessary to constitute them a particular Congregational Church, and this political union or essential form is a visible covenant, agreement or consent, whereby they give up themselves to the Lord to the observing of the ordinances of Christ together in the same society; so a visible political union between us as churches is necessary to constitute us one particular Congregational Church:

Wherefore, we, the Second and Fourth Churches of Ipswich, having agreed to become one united Church of Jesus Christ for the worship of God and the observing of his ordinances together in the same society, and having before as distinct churches covenanted with God and one another in a distinct covenant respectively, do now as churches, consistent with sacred regard thereto, covenant together to be one church of Jesus Christ, and solemnly renew covenant with God in Christ to walk and worship together as one body, by signing together the following form or covenant*

---

*This covenant which is given in the church records is there stated to have been taken verbatim from the covenant framed by Rev. Mr. Higginson, for the church in Salem, Aug. 6, 1829; with the omission of one paragraph, and the addition of two paragraphs and two clauses.

which is in substance the same as is understood to be the original covenant of the Second Church of Ipswich, in which it (that is the Second Church) was founded.

"In testimony of our holy resolution in the strength of Christ to stand and walk together in the fellowship of the Gospel, in a careful observance of this covenant and the foregoing heads of agreement, we not only call Heaven and Earth to witness, but set our names hereunto, in the presence of an Ecclesiastical Council, this 26th day of October, 1774."

The record proceeds:

"It was then desired that if any of the congregation had aught to object to the articles, they would signify it. There was no objection. Thereupon the moderator, in the name and by the unanimous vote of the council, saluted the brethren as a united church by the name of the Second Church in Ipswich, and gave the right hand of fellowship to them as a sister church; also gave the right hand of fellowship to the Rev. Mr. Cleaveland, as Pastor of the united church, and the other Elders of the Council did the same. The united church voted their thanks to the Council, and the business of the day was concluded with singing the one hundred and thirty-third and a part of the one hundred and twenty-second Psalms, and with prayer by the moderator."

As this very year the church had for the first time voted "to choose some of the brethren skilled in singing, to lead the church and congregation in the service of singing praise to God"—instead of the lining of the hymns by one of the deacons—and such men as Joseph Perkins, John Choate and Abraham Perkins were the first choristers, it is not to be doubted that those Psalms extolling fraternal union and praying for the peace of Jerusalem were sung with great musical skill and fervor.

The legal union of the two parishes under the name of the Second Parish was effected the next year, by conditions of union adopted by them both, March 2, 1775, and an act of the General Court passed on their petition, April 10th.

To Mr. Cleaveland, in his successful accomplishment of this so desirable but difficult undertaking, could properly be applied the prophecy of Isaiah: "Thou shalt raise up the foundations of many generations; and thou shalt be called the repairer of the breach, the restorer of paths to dwell in."

Most fully merited was the tribute paid to his memory for this beneficent work, by Rev. Dr. Parish of Byfield in his memorial discourse preached not long after Mr. Cleaveland's death:

That Mr. Cleaveland was *** *** *** *** *** *** irreproachable *** *** *** *** *** *** of *** which *** *** ***
***

At first he was *** *** *** *** *** of the *** *** probably both, possessing the *** *** *** *** might *** *** *** *** to *** *** *** *** *** *** *** *** *** the *** the darkness of *** *** *** *** *** *** *** *** ***

REV. MR. CLEAVELAND'S CHAPLAINCIES.

3. The third kind of service which Mr. Cleaveland rendered the community was in his military chaplaincies. Like his eminent predecessor, Rev. Mr. Wise, he served his country in this office in two wars, with a sincere and fearless patriotism.

In the French and Indian War (1756–1763) he was commissioned March 13, 1758, on the staff of Gen. Bagley of the Third Provincial Regiment of Foot, the fourth company of which was made up of Chebacco and Hamilton men, officers and privates, in the army of Gen. Abercrombie, which was to attempt the capture of Fort Ticonderoga. Travelling on horseback Mr. C. joined his regiment at Albany, and was with it on the northward march early in June, to and across Lake George; in the bloody and disastrous fight which followed, on the 8th, not far from its northwest shore, in an attempt to force the intrenchments of the French posted there; in its retreat; and during the remainder of the season until autumn. Obtaining a furlough, he returned home in October.

The next summer his regiment was ordered to reinforce the garrison occupying the fortress of Louisburg on the island of Cape Breton, (which had been taken in 1758), during the operations of Gen. Wolfe against Quebec. Mr. Cleaveland, "much affected by the parting scene with wife and children," as he writes, sailed from Boston, July 14, on the sloop *Wilmot*, Capt. Gay, and because of fogs, calms and headwinds had a voyage of fourteen days to the island. There he was occupied with his duties as chaplain until, Quebec having fallen and the troops having been ordered back to New England, he started on his return voyage, Oct. 30, 1759 and arrived in Boston, Nov. 9.

During these absences his pulpit was supplied a part of the time by neighboring ministers. Often there was no preaching, but a meeting was held every Sabbath and prayers were always offered for the pastor and the soldiers.

Not only is the sea-chest he took with him on this expedition preserved in the Essex Institute at Salem, together with his commission signed by Gov. Pownall, but also his journal and letters; from which we learn quite fully of his preaching and his private exhortations to the soldiers, his ministering to them when sick, sending their messages home, and communicating to their friends tidings of their welfare, sometimes of their sickness and death; his lamentations over the profanity and other vices prevalent in the army, and various experiences of camp and garrison life. On the voyage he had prayers night and morning, and he reports a great reformation from swearing, among the crew, through his expostulations with them. The editor of that portion of the Journal, which has been published in the Historical Collections of the Essex Institute, fitly remarks:

"These journals abundantly show also that he knew how to mingle on terms the most friendly with men whose habits of life and thought had always been very different from his own. It is impossible to doubt that the British nobleman, the English colonel, and even the Church of England clergyman, with whom he then and there came in contact, fully appreciated and readily acknowledged the solid worth of this poor, but brave, Yankee, Puritan, Congregational Minister."

A few extracts from his journal and the Louisburg letters to his wife, which have never before been printed, are as follows:

"I need help from above to be wise and faithful. I desire you and all the christian friends to pray for me, that I may be a fisher of men, and may cast the net on the right side of the ship."

Aug. 22. "I live very comfortably here, but not so agreeably as in my own family with my best friends. But I doubt not on the leave of my being called by Providence to be here as yet. And O, that my being here may not be in vain, but that God would own and bless me, and make me a blessing to many ready to perish. Profane swearing seems to be the naturalized language of the Regulars in general. Last Lord's day I preached from the words of Christ, 'But I say unto you, swear not at all.' We had a very crowded assembly, vastly more Regulars than Provincials. My Lord Rollo, the Governor's Lieut. Col., was present."

"One thing looks encouraging, that every time we meet we are more and more thronged, and last Sabbath in the afternoon, the house was crowded quite full, half an hour before the bell rang, and it was said that in the time of worship, as many stood around the house, as were within; and to appearance they gave very earnest attention. But nothing will be efficacious, unless the arm of the Lord is revealed and the Divine Spirit poured out. O pray for me, and let my people know, as you have opportunity, that I desire they would continue instant in prayer for me. And give my kind regards to all the ministers that are so good as to preach for me in my absence, and let them know it is my earnest desire they would pray much for me and stir up the godly, as they have opportunity to do the same."

Sept. 2. "I am not without hopes that God will bless my labors in Louisburg, especially among the Regulars. The seats in the meeting-house are commonly filled with them before the Provincials get there, and they give such good attention."

On the Sabbath after the news of the taking of Quebec was received, Mr. Cleaveland "preached on the occasion of the recent victory to a full and solemn house." The Sabbath following, Oct. 14, he "preached to a very crowded house indeed." The 15th was "a day of rejoicing over the victories at Quebec. The weather was greatly like winter." On the 19th "the rejoicing still continued." Oct. 25th was observed as a day of religious thanksgiving and Mr. C. again preached to the garrison, from Heb. 13, 13.

On the voyage home he wrote:

"Nov. 4. (Sabbath). There was no walking on deck on account of the roughness of the sea. Met a little privateer with English colors; hailed her, but she made no answer. One or two other ships made their appearance and hoisted the red flag, and we the blue. At 4 p.m., we saw land along shore for several leagues. After filling, tacking and floating, the wind sprang up at midnight, much in our favor."

"Nov. 8th. A fine breeze, pleasant weather, and hopes of soon getting home. The Lord be praised for such a favorable breeze."

"Nov. 9th. Fair wind still continuing—good dinner. We ran well until sunrise, than it began to rain. The light is ahead, but the wind dies away and we move slowly. However, by gentle breaths we arrived at Boston, and cast anchor by 3 o'clock, p.m."

"Nov. 11th. (Sabbath). Went to Mr. Bowles' and dined, then crossed Charlestown ferry, got a horse and did not get down from it, until I reached my own door, where I found my family well. Thanks to the Most High God, for his good hand over me, in returning me in safety. What shall I render to God for all his benefits toward me? God grant me grace to walk answerable to the mercies I have received. Amen and Amen."

In the earliest preparations for armed resistance to Great Britain near the close of 1774, Chebacco was on the alert to do its part. Of the meeting held Dec. 20, for organizing a military company of foot, at which sixty-eight men signed the muster-roll of the "Training Band," Mr. Cleaveland was the clerk. And the strong probability is, both from their sentiment and phraseology, that the courageous and patriotic "Resolutions" passed at that meeting and preserved in his hand-writing, were drawn up by him. Two of these are as follows:

"2. *Resolved:* That the officers, who shall be chosen and shall accept of the choice, shall hold themselves obliged, in obedience to their superior Officers appointed agreeable to the advice of the Provincial Congress, to send us forth to action in the Field of Battle in Defence of our constitutional privileges, whensoever there shall be a manifest call for it against our common enemies."

"4. *Resolved:* That we will yield such Obedience to the commands of the Officers that shall be chosen and shall accept of the choice, as the Provincial Laws respecting the Militia require: and submit to such punishments, in case of Delinquency in us, as the said Laws also require."

After the Lexington and Concord fight we find Mr. Cleaveland at Watertown, June 1, to tender to the leaders such services as he could render, and the next month acting as chaplain of Col. Little's regiment, the 17th Foot, Continental army (enlisted July 1), with his quarters in Hollis Hall, one of the College buildings at Cambridge; his youngest son, a boy of sixteen, as his attendant and his three other sons and his two brothers (one a Colonel) also among the host gathered about Boston. A few of his letters of this time are extant.

Aug. 28, he writes to Dr. N. Daggett, President of Yale College:

"An unnatural war! We hear its confused noises and see garments rolled in blood. Yesterday the cannon roared all day long from both sides. Two of our men killed, one wounded. We killed some of the enemy; sunk one of their floating batteries and disabled another. Our people in high spirits and extremely impatient to be at the enemy. This moment the drums are beating an alarm. It is said the enemy are coming out. I wish they would, but doubt about their having courage to leave their lines to attempt to force ours."

Obliged to return to his parochial duties, he writes, Nov. 28, 1775, from Chebacco to his three sons, John, Parker and Ebenezer, who were then in the Army:

"I hope you are all well. Our love is to you all; wish you to write and let me know what is passing in the army, and your circumstances. I don't know when I shall come again to the army. The weather is such that I cannot perform the duties of a chaplain abroad, if I was present. It is somewhat likely I shall come week after next."

Dec. 8, he writes that he is going to camp as soon as his surtout is made.

Dec. 10, 1775. To his son John, he writes:

"I suppose your campaign is now expired and your face set homeward. But I hope you will soon return to the help of the Lord against the mighty. God has done great things for us by sea and by land, since we have engaged in defence of our rights; and though the wickedness of the army is great, I hope and believe that God will plead our cause; but the wicked he will punish for their wickedness. The Lord keep me, my brother, and our sons from having any fellowship with the unfruitful works of darkness, but that we rather reprove them and be made instrumental of procuring temporal salvation for the land, and be made subjects ourselves of eternal salvation."

To Col. Phinney he writes:

"Chebacco, Dec. 13, 1775. Dear Sir. By reason of the coldness of the weather being such that I could not perform Divine service abroad in the open air at camp, I have been at home for some time. I shall come to camp again shortly, but don't expect to tarry in winter season, for the above mentioned reason." "It grieves me that there is so much profaneness in our army. I should think officers might do much to suppress it, and trust there is not so much in your regiment as in those where some of the chief officers don't set the best example before their men, relative to it; yet I hope God will appear for us, ere the spring comes."

In the autumn of 1776 when the militia were called out to protect the frontiers of Connecticut and aid in guarding supplies, Mr. Cleaveland again took the position of chaplain, in the Third Essex Regiment commanded by his young parishioner and friend, Col. Jonathan Cogswell, and containing the Chebacco company of over sixty men, among them the chaplain's youngest son. The regiment marched from home Sept. 25th and was stationed for a time at Fairfield on the Sound. Mr. Cleaveland joined it Oct. 9th, on the 15th wrote to his son Parker as follows:

"I arrived six days ago in health and found Nehemiah and all our Ipswich company in health; and the little army, stationed in this town consisting of two regiments is in general in very good health and behaves well. We hear no profaneness amongst them and they attend divine service in the meeting house night and morning very cheerfully and seriously, to all appearance."

The regiment was also in the battle of White Plains, Oct. 28th, in which though many were killed and wounded on both sides, the British failed of their object, which was to get possession of the eastern roads and cut off supplies. After occupying post with most of the New England troops under Gen. Lee at North Castle, the regiment was ordered home early in the winter, when New Jersey had become the chief seat of war.

Unable at his age to endure the exposures to health, of life in camp and on the march, or even to be absent from his parish for any great length of time, by the example he had already given as well as by his words he inspired his sons with a patriotic spirit and gave them to his country.

The oldest, Lieut. John Cleaveland, served through the whole war, and was the rest of his life a faithful soldier of Jesus Christ in the gospel ministry. Ebenezer was first a private in the army, afterwards served on a privateer, was taken prisoner, exchanged or liberated, and died of fever on board a continental ship on his return home from the West Indies.*

The other two were also in the service for a considerable time, one as surgeon-in-chief of a Continental regiment. Afterwards through long lives they were among the most eminent physicians of their day in Essex county, serving also with marked ability and influence in public life — both of them often in the Legislature, one in the State and United States constitutional conventions, and the other a judge and afterwards chief justice of the Court of Sessions for a long period. They were both conscientious christian men of strong religious convictions.

---

*Respecting his death Mr. Cleaveland wrote a characteristic and touching letter to another of his sons, which is in part as follows:

"Chebacco, April 28, 1780. My dear Son. How fading are all things here below! On Friday last we had the heavy and certain news of the death of your brother Ebenezer. He dyed, according to Capt. Odle's book, the 30th of March, on board the continental ship *Eustis*, Capt. Samuel Bishop, in latitude 25°, coming home from Eustatia, last. The Captain said your brother rejoiced, or was glad the time of his departure had come. Capt. Odle and several others said Ebenezer had his reason to the last, but was not able to speak much the day he died. Your brother being dead yet speaketh and preacheth a lecture 'Be ye also ready' — louder than ever your father preached, or than ever we heard thunder roar. Oh that it may touch the heart to the centre and rouse up all the powers of the soul! to what? Why to be still and know that the Supreme Being is God, and to glorify him as God, by a life of faith in him and obedience to Christ, who is the head over *all things*, and does all things *well*. Let us think and *speak* well of him and of *all* his administration in providence and grace."

A remark sometimes made by aged persons, seventy years ago, who remembered the days of the Revolution, that he "preached all the men of his parish into the army and then went himself," also attests Mr. Cleaveland's zeal for the cause as well as his great influence over the people of Chebacco. And so what his eulogist, Dr. Parish, declared after his death was literally true:

> "Active and enterprising, he repeatedly left the silence of his study for the din of war; the joys of domestic peace for the dangers of the bloody field. The waters of Champlain, the rocks of Cape Breton, the fields of Cambridge and the banks of the Hudson listened to the fervor of his addresses."*

And his patriotic example, together with his preaching, helps us more clearly to understand why President John Adams once said to a French statesman, that "American independence was mainly due to the clergy."

Such was Mr. Cleaveland's zeal in his religious work; and such his services in uniting the two Chebacco churches and in his two army chaplaincies.

REV. MR. CLEAVELAND'S LATER YEARS.

The remaining years of the century after the war of Independence was over, he seems to have passed in quiet and serenity, dwelling among his own people, like a sort of patriarch, active and energetic to the last in all the duties of his ministerial calling.

In 1790 the pleasant relations between him and his parish were illustrated by their movement to build a new and comparatively costly meeting house. This they completed within about three years and on the 8th of October 1793 he had the great satisfaction of preaching to a large audience the dedication sermon, from Acts x: 33.

---

*Mr. Cleaveland's Revolutionary camp-chest is in the Essex Institute; and the rude buck-horn handled sword, which he wore in all his campaigns, has been preserved and is now in the possession of one of his descendants.

It was not until about this time that hymns began to be read by the minister in the Sabbath worship, as they are now; and not until about five years earlier than this that choirs began to do the singing. On this occasion, "the singing was conducted with great animation and power, the choir being led by Mr. Isaac Long of Hopkinton, N. H., one of the builders of the meeting-house."

In this edifice, also, Mr. Cleaveland preached, March 8, 1797, a half-century lecture from Acts xxvi: 22; which he concluded with these words:

> I am now near the close of the seventy-fifth year of my age, and have especial reason with uniform gratitude to the Supreme Disposer of all good events, to say: 'Having obtained help of God I continue unto this day.' For near fifty-five years since, while at college, I was taken sick of a violent fever, which deprived me of my reason and ran high up n me for forty days; and for near a fortnight my life was despaired of by my attendants and all who saw me. Even the President of the college was so apprehensive of my dying then, that he prepared a funeral sermon to be preached on account of my expected decease. But in the moment of extremity the Lord appeared and plucked me as a brand from the burning, and having obtained help of God I continue unto this time, to my surprise as often as I think of it. While that president and two presidents besides, and a large number of my fellow-students are gone to their long home. And this day, fifty years ago I was ordained a pastor of a flock of Christ in this place, and here have continued to preach the gospel half a century."

That Mr. Cleaveland, with all his influence among his people, never arrogated to himself any authority over them, but continued to the last to recognize the supremacy of the brotherhood and the responsibility resting upon them in all ecclesiastical matters, (things which it has been aptly said are "fundamental in the constitution of Congregational churches, and essential to the success of this form of church polity,") is well illustrated by a vote of the church of April 30, 1797 on receiving an invitation to join other churches in an ordaining council. It was voted to comply with the invitation but not to choose a delegate, "until the church should hear the candidate preach a sermon or two." Having, May 28th, heard him preach "to good acceptance three sermons," they chose their delegate, both they and their pastor, then as always, considering the participation of the church in such an affair to be no mere form, but a transaction in which the whole body was a responsible party.

Living on still longer and completing the fifty-second year of his ministry and the seventy-seventh of his life, and on the last Sabbath but one before the end preaching with his usual animation, he died on the twenty-second of April 1799, coming to his grave *in a full age, like as a shock of corn cometh in, in his season.*

After such a career, "eminently a faithful watchman, being ever ready and apt to teach," *an eloquent man and mighty in the Scriptures, full of faith and of the Holy Ghost,* as he had been, no wonder that Rev. Mr. Dana of Ipswich took for the text of his funeral sermon the cry of Elisha at the translation of Elijah: "My father, my father, the chariot of Israel and the horsemen thereof."

And most fitly did the Rev. Dr. Parish of Byfield, in his memorial discourse from Psalms cxvi: 15, delivered in the deceased pastor's pulpit on the second of June following, rise to a lofty strain of glowing eulogy in his appreciative delineation of the character of his venerated elder in the ministry.

With the published descriptions of Mr. Cleaveland's personal appearance all are familiar,—his erect muscular form, his stature of nearly six feet, his florid complexion and blue eyes, his amiable and benevolent face into which every body loved to look. According to his own memorandum he weighed in 1769 two hundred and seven pounds, and in 1773 two hundred and thirty pounds. He was a man of strong constitution and ardent temperament; his voice heavy and of great compass.

One of his younger contemporaries said of Mr. Cleaveland as a preacher and writer:

"An earnest spirit, an unpolished energy and a sincerity which none could question characterized him in the pulpit. His familiarity with the Scriptures was proverbial; his general learning respectable. His writings though often forcible and fervent could lay no claim to elegance."

One of his descendants refers to some of the most prominent qualities of his character in these words: "An earnest and honest man, conscientious, faithful and affectionate, acting and speaking always under a high sense of duty and throwing his whole heart into everything he said or did."

III. The last, and of course the briefest, division of this historical review has to do with the present century, a period less eventful than the two preceding, but, in decided contrast with them, distinguished on the whole for calm, steady, spiritual progress, and for the great activity of the church in all good works, the successive pastors preeminently zealous and leading the way but the brotherhood cooperating, and exercising their varied gifts for the same end.

Out of all that has taken place during this period two things at least should be specified as conspicuously characterizing the life of the church, and therefore as worthy of record.

1. As has been true everywhere else in New England, this has been in this community, on the whole, emphatically the era of seasons of special and sometimes intense but thoughtful and rational religious interest.

Because we do not find any such revivals taking place in the two *earliest* pastorates of the century, that of Rev. Josiah Webster, extending from Nov. 13, 1799 to July 23, 1806, and that of Rev. Thomas Holt from Jan. 25, 1809 to April 20, 1813, it would be an unwarrantable inference and most uncharitable to impute any lack of faithfulness or of pious earnestness to these ministers. The condition of the times, just then, was most unfavorable to the spiritual life and prosperity of society everywhere. Some of the demoralizing influences resulting from the Revolutionary war and from contact with French infidelity still remained; political party spirit, the animosity between Federalists and Republicans, was intense, exceedingly bitter and often personal; there was great excitement throughout the land occasioned by the encroachments of England upon the rights and interests of this nation, increasing from the noted attack upon the *Chesapeake* in 1807, down to their culmination in 1812, and the outbreak of war; and in part as a consequence of this state of things, the churches generally were in a condition of stagnation and deadness.

Through the preaching of some Christian Baptist ministers in the south part of the town, beginning with 1805, and the interest awakened in their meetings, (which resulted in the formation of the Christian society in 1808), our parish was somewhat weakened, and the congregation diminished in numbers, near the close of Mr. Webster's pastorate.

REV. MR. WEBSTER'S PASTORATE.

We have however the testimony of some of those who were his parishioners, that he was an acceptable and interesting preacher, a zealous christian leader, exerting all his energies for the promotion of godliness in the community and greatly beloved by his church and people.

At Mr. Webster's settlement here there were forty-seven members of the church, only thirteen of whom were men, several of these quite advanced in years, and one of them a non-resident.

One of these aged disciples was Dea. Jonathan Cogswell, at that time seventy-four years old, who died in 1812 aged eighty-six. Another of just about the same age was Capt. Aaron Foster, a soldier at the taking of Louisbourg in 1745 and a member of the church from the year 1763, who lived to the age of eighty-seven.

Almost the only other man active in religious matters was Dea. Grover Dodge, a native of Hamilton but a resident of this town from his youth, always and universally respected as a citizen, a convert in the great revival of 1763, acting as deacon from 1812 till 1821 and later, a consistent christian, 'an Israelite indeed in whom was no guile,' through a long life which ended in 1831.

Among the substantial and influential men *in the parish* in this earlier part of the century, mention should be made in particular of three. One of these was Mr. David Choate, a soldier in the Revolution, always deeply interested in the cause of education and a successful school teacher, and often chosen to fill places of responsibility and trust as a man of unswerving integrity and weight of character. Though not a member of the church, he gave during the latter part of his life strong evidence of possessing a genuine christian spirit. Soon after his death in 1808 at the age of fifty-one, Dr. Mussey wrote:

"Mr. Choate was a man of uncommon intellectual endowments. Though denied the advantages of a regular education he arrived at a degree of improvement often unattained by men of the first opportunities, and possessed talents which would have been an honor to a statesman. In the social circle none were his superiors. He lived the friend and supporter of virtue and order, and died in hope of a happier state through the mercy of a Redeemer."

Another was Col. Jonathan Cogswell, Sen., an officer in the Revolution, who died in 1819 at the age of seventy-nine. A sketch of him written soon after his death describes him as

"A useful citizen and magistrate, a devout christian and an excellent man. In public life he manifested a sound judgment and unshaken integrity and executed every trust with scrupulous fidelity. Free from all appearance of selfishness, the happiness of others seemed the study of his life. His religion, as it had been the guide of his youth, became the comfort of his age. The poor man's gratitude acknowledged his benevolence and the uniform uprightness of his department declared his fervent piety."

Still a third was George Choate, Esq., a man who also gave his hearty and constant support to the institutions of religion; and who held various parish offices—that of treasurer for a number of years ending with his death in 1826, when he was at the age of sixty-four. As a citizen, magistrate, town-officer and legislator he deservedly enjoyed the highest confidence and respect of his fellow-townsmen; and his name has been perpetuated and adorned by his son, Dr. George Choate the eminent physician in Salem for a long period, and by his still more distinguished grandsons of the same profession and at the bar, of the present generation.

During Mr. Webster's seven years' ministry, twenty-one persons united with the church. One of the eight men was Dr. Reuben D. Mussey, a graduate of Dartmouth College in 1803 and engaged in the practice of medicine here from 1805 through 1808, who filled for a time the office of church clerk and was a member of the Sabbath choir — a skilful player upon the bass-viol. The late President Lord of Dartmouth College wrote of him:

> "He was sometimes brusque in his manner, but he had heavenly music in his soul. A discord or an untimely movement fretted him. But when, as sometimes in the congregation or the social circle, a glorious harmony went up, then the strain rose from his, as if impassioned viol, in enlivening concert; and his chastened spirit seemed to go with it, into communion with the choir above."

After further special study in Philadelphia and the prosecution of his profession in Salem five years, he was a professor in the Medical Schools of Dartmouth and Bowdoin Colleges and at Cincinnati, O., in succession. He then founded and lectured in the Miami Medical School six years; and after thus spending forty-six years in medical instruction lived in retirement in Boston until his death in 1866, at the age of eighty-six.

It is certainly an interesting fact to us and to this community which he several times revisited in his later life, that this eminent physician, among the foremost in his profession in scientific knowledge and skill, began his religious life, a young man of twenty-five years of age, while practising his profession in this parish; that such a surgeon, attaining a national reputation, "who" as his biographer — a distinguished medical professor—states, "believed much in skilled surgery, something in nature but most of all in God, so that on the eve of a great operation he frequently knelt at the bed-side of the patient and sought skill and strength and success from the great source of all vitality," first bowed the knee in social prayer with the members, few though they were, of this Chebacco church; that the strong and noble character of the man, whom the same writer describes as "a devoted member and officer of the church all his days, a constant observer of the Sabbath, an earnest defender and propagator of the faith, a gratuitous adviser and benefactor of the poor," was nurtured in its early unfolding and growth under the influences of the sanctuary and the people of God in this village.

Two others who were active, working members of the church, forsaking not the ways of Zion, in those days when few came to her solemn feasts, were Mr. John Mears, a native of Chebacco (born June 20, 1777), converted under Mr. Webster's preaching, steadfast and faithful in sustaining the social religious meetings of the church, keeping up almost to the time of his death, (Sept. 7, 1865 at the age of eighty-eight), his regular attendance upon the Sabbath services though in his later years totally blind, exceedingly painstaking in the religious training of his children,—all but one of the ten of them who reached maturity entering the church in their early years,— and Mr. Nathan Burnham, a man of very much the same stamp, quiet and undemonstrative but a pillar in the sacred temple, not often making exhortations but frequently taking part very acceptable in the devotional exercises of church-meetings, especially active in times of religious interest later on, and a deacon from 1821 until his death in 1860 at the age of eighty-four.

All honor to the memory of these few who guarded and bore onward the ark of the Lord, almost alone, down to about the year 1815, when the voice of war was again hushed and peace reigned throughout our borders.

THE REVIVALS OF RELIGION.

Prior to that date we have record of only three marked and extensive revivals of religion in the entire history of the church,—in 1727, 1741 and 1763—which have been already mentioned.

Of the six of which the community has had experience since then, four took place during the pastorate of Rev. Robert Crowell which extended forty-one years, from Aug. 10, 1814, when there were only six male members of the church and thirty-two in all, to his death, Nov. 10, 1855.

On the third of the next January after his ordination the church voted to hold a meeting on the first Tuesday in every month for prayer and religious conversation, at the house of the pastor, at which some of the topics considered were: "the nature and duty of prayer," "the church covenant as a rule of duty," and "the importance of religious instruction for children and youth."

From the church records it appears that the very next month after that, some religious interest began to manifest itself which continued more than two years; one or two persons at least, (not members of the church) attending at many of the meetings for religious conversation or to relate their experience and ask admission to the church. Under date of March 10, 1816, mention is made of the admission of two persons to the church and the record reads:

"The assembly appears solemn. May the Lord sanctify the solemn scene to the conviction and conversion of others."

And under date of June 3d:

"The church met to unite in the general concert of prayer, as well as for mutual conversation. A few present not church members, who conversed on the state of their minds, some of them under concern, and some having obtained a hope though not free from all doubt. The Lord grant that a plentiful shower may succeed these mercy drops."

The number of persons gathered into the church during this time up to June, 1817 was nineteen. Whether the six admitted to the church in the two years following should also be reckoned among the fruits of this first revival, I am unable to say.

One of those who united with the church in 1817 was Capt. Samuel Burnham (born Oct. 28, 1787) who was superintendent of the Sabbath School from 1818 till 1857, and ever after a teacher in it, was the treasurer of the church from 1821 till 1858, was elected deacon in 1828 and served in that office until his death Nov. 18, 1873, at the age of eighty-six. For a long series of years he regularly conducted the Sabbath morning prayer-meeting in the chapel and the Tuesday evening meeting from the first establishment of those services, and never failed in untiring devotion and efficiency in the discharge of these and all the many responsible trusts assigned to him by the church,—a sincere, useful, godly man.

The *second* of these periods of special religious interest began in September, 1827 and (like its predecessor) immediately after a special meeting of the church, on the first Sabbath evening of that month, to pray for the effusion of the Holy Spirit. It continued about nine months. Before the end of the first month the church clerk entered this minute upon the records: "Such an attention to the things of eternity has become apparent, as has not been witnessed within the memory of any but the aged." And in May, 1828, he made record that "the Sabbath morning prayer meeting, the Thursday evening lecture, the inquiry and church prayer-meetings on Tuesday evening, and either public or private prayer-meetings on Saturday evening are all maintained and with much interest, solemnity and feeling;" and during this and the two following years more than eighty persons united with the church, a large majority of them young married men and women, who constituted to a very great extent the working force of the church for the next thirty years.

Among them all, mention may perhaps be properly made by name of Capt. Francis Burnham, to whom the spiritual change of that revival brought a revolution in religious belief and the beginning of a life of most unvarying devotion to duty. In the use of his vigorous powers of mind and his possessions alike, he realized in an unusual degree the idea of stewardship to his divine Master. A diligent student of the Bible, giving daily and earnest thought to its teachings, his intellectual gifts were exercised in the Sabbath School, and often in the prayer-meeting, with great interest and profit to those who listened.

A prosperous man through close attention to his business, he was conscientiously and heartily liberal in giving of his substance to all worthy charitable objects, and especially to Home and Foreign missions; and from a moderate estate, he left at his death in legacies to ten different benevolent societies the sum of $11,000 in all, besides $500 each to this church and parish.

Always at his post of Christian service he used the office of a deacon well, being found blameless, from his election to it in 1834, until his death Sept. 16, 1871, at the age of eighty years and eleven months.

Another of those who entered upon the religious life at that time was Mr. John Choate, a man always devoted to the interests of the parish, sometimes serving it in responsible trusts, widely known to the community, as was written of him soon after his death, Oct. 18, 1863, "for his great originality of character, for his integrity and sterling value as a public man as well as for the virtues which adorned his private life." Though, through a certain diffidence, not much given to public speaking of any kind, he was a man of decided Christian principle, who reflected much and deeply upon the great truths of revelation and derived the strongest consolation from the faith he professed, to the end of his life. One of his striking remarks once made to a friend, was that "as he sometimes stood and looked upon the broad sheet of water adjoining the islands which constituted his farm, in some calm morning when the whole surface was like a mirror, it gave him, as he thought, a good idea of the full ocean of God's love, in which the soul of the Christian would lave itself after the winds and storms of life were over."

The *third* revival was in 1839 when about twenty-five persons were hopefully converted; and the *fourth*, in the years 1849 and 1850, in which about thirty were brought into the church, most of them members of the Sabbath School; and of this spiritual harvest the seed was apparently the Assembly's Catechism, in a thorough study of which large numbers had been spending the preceding summer, learning by heart this summary of Christian doctrine for the prize of a bible offered by the church.

The *fifth* of this series of revivals occurred in the year 1857, soon after the beginning of the ministry of Rev. James M. Bacon, who,—after a pastorate in Littleton from 1846 to 1849, and in Amesbury from 1851 to 1855—was installed over this church July 6, 1856.

"Entering upon this pastorate," writes Rev. Dr. Wellman, "at the age of thirty-eight, matured in christian character by protracted and severe discipline, enriched in the knowledge of Christ and his gospel and in that pastoral wisdom which can come only from long experience in dealing with all classes of people, he was fitted, as never before, for the work of the christian ministry. Without any parade of plans or promises, he met his people face to face, and talked to them plainly and earnestly, as became a man sent from God, 'of sin and of righteousness and of judgment.' It was like 'the voice of one crying in the wilderness, Prepare ye the way of the Lord.' He was emphatically a preacher of righteousness; at the same time he tenderly pointed his hearers to Christ, and assured them, as if they had never heard the message before, that they could become reconciled to God and be saved only as they accepted Jesus as their Lord and Saviour. And soon the spiritual power of his labors was manifest; all classes were moved, and during the winter and spring of the second year of his pastorate the town was blessed with a powerful revival of religion. About fifty persons, converts in this revival, united with the church."[*]

Of Mr. Bacon's interest in young men and his influence in leading several of them to devote themselves to the Chris-

---

[*] Biographical sketch by Rev. J. W. Wellman, D.D., in *The Congregational Quarterly*, Vol. xvii, No. 3.

tian ministry, of his patriotic zeal and his prayers for the sons of his people in the army, in the war of the Rebellion, or of the ardent piety, the singleness of aim, the self-sacrificing devotion, the honest and faithful preaching of this servant of Christ, you have no need that I speak, for it is all in your memories and your hearts.

On account of ill health, Mr. Bacon closed his labors here July 8, 1869. He was afterwards pastor of the church in Ashby from 1870 until his death March 5, 1873.

The ministers of the church since Mr. Bacon's dismission have been Rev. Darius A. Moorehouse, installed June 30, 1870, and dismissed Sept. 14, 1874; Rev. Edward G. Smith, installed July 15, 1875, and dismissed Feb. 8, 1877; Rev. John L. Harris, acting pastor for one year from May 1, 1877; Rev. Francis H. Boynton, installed Dec. 11, 1879, and dismissed May 18, 1882; Rev. Frank H. Palmer, acting pastor since Oct. 1, 1882.

The *sixth* and most recent revival of this century took place during the pastorate of Rev. Mr. Smith, in 1875-6, and brought into the church forty-one members.

2. The second thing especially noticeable in the history of this church and parish, during the last seventy years, is the religious activity of their members in a great variety of ways, a few of which it may be proper to enumerate.

One instance of the outworking of this spirit of religious enterprise, we find, in the provision made in 1820 for a suitable place (which down to that time had been lacking) for the social religious meetings and other gatherings of the church and society. For this purpose some members of the parish,—prominent among whom were Messrs. Joseph Choate, John Dexter and William Andrews, Jr.,—took upon themselves the care and expense of erecting a chapel, which was dedicated with appropriate religious services in December of that year.

In one of its rooms adapted to that use, the liberality of

others deposited, the very next year, a church library which had its beginning in 1815 in one hundred volumes of books presented by a number of donors to the church. This gradually increased in size until it numbered more than two hundred volumes of standard theological and other religious works and was for many years a source of much interest and instruction to a considerable portion of the members of the church.

INTEREST IN MISSIONS.

In this building also, from the first opening of it, was held the monthly missionary concert, (which had been omitted for some time for want of a convenient place to meet in and which just about the year 1820 began to be observed generally in the churches), and the meetings of a society organized in 1826 for the special support of the cause of missions.

Following if not directly stimulated by this development of an interest in christian work among the heathen was the awakening of a deeper regard for Home missions, leading to practical efforts for the cultivation of waste places near at hand. To the establishment and support of the Congregational churches in Lanesville and Gloucester Harbor liberal contributions were statedly made for a long period.

Many "shares," as the gifts in money were called, were taken in the new meeting-house in West Gloucester in 1833; and to the newly organized church there, which consisted at first only of women, two of our members, Messrs. John Choate and John S. Burnham were regularly dismissed to become its deacons. They officiated in that capacity several years, until, through the blessing of God upon that Home missionary endeavor in the increase of that church, their services were no longer required.

For the promotion of various Christian objects that chapel proved an exceedingly serviceable structure for twenty years, until the remodeling of the meeting-house in 1842 furnished more commodious apartments for these same ends.

Another illustration of this forwardness for religious work which prevailed, and of the steadfastness in it, is found in a vote of the church in a time of religious interest in 1828, appointing a large committee to go forth two by two, to visit the families of the parish, for the purpose of conversing with them on the necessity of giving immediate attention to the subject of religion, and a vote a few days later that the whole church be a committee for that purpose; as also in the canvassing of the town in 1835 to see what proportion of the inhabitants attended no religious meeting on the Sabbath.

THE TUESDAY EVENING PRAYER MEETING.

But it especially appears in the establishment, in 1828, of the Tuesday evening prayer-meeting, held at the houses of many of the church members in turn, in different parts of the parish, for a long series of years, and of late in the conference room of the church.

This meeting, sustained wholly by laymen already for upwards of half a century, has certainly a remarkable record, as regards the vigor with which it has been for the most part sustained, the wide range of doctrinal and practical topics discussed in it, the freedom, ability and originality with which they were often handled, the suggestive, stimulating and edifying thoughts expressed, the fervent prayers offered, and its usefulness in feeding the flame of christian feeling and nourishing the spiritual life of the church. In all these and manifold other ways it has been accomplishing a great and excellent work; and many who have attended owe more than can be described to the fathers and brothers, among the dead and the living, who have been the indefatigable upholders and the shining lights of this social Christian meeting for devotion and conference.

THE TEMPERANCE MOVEMENT.

Still a third form of this activity of the brotherhood appeared at the beginning of the Temperance movement in 1829. When, after an address in the meeting-house July 16, there was a call to organize the Essex Temperance Society on the principle of total abstinence, seven persons besides the minister responded with their signatures to the pledge; whose names, were Winthrop Low (the first president), Samuel Burnham, John Choate, John Perkins, Jonathan Eveleth, Francis Burnham and David Choate, all members of this parish, and all but one, members of the church. Within a year following, besides the twenty-nine ladies who enrolled their names, there were eleven men, all of this parish, and all but two of them, church members, who also signed the pledge.

Although at first there was strong and bitter opposition, the members of the society were full of zeal; they procured lecturers on the subject and carried the reform steadily onward, until public sentiment was completely revolutionized. As early as 1833, so great was its influence, that the town voted "no license;" and soon an advance was made to abstinence from fermented liquors.

THE SABBATH SCHOOL.

By far the most important kind of practical work, however, in which the Christian spirit of a large number of the men and women of this church has found scope for its exercise, has been the teaching of the Scriptures and the religious training of the children and youth in the Sabbath school, which was first established in 1814 but the conduct of which was for so long a period of time in the hands of Hon. David Choate.*

A deacon in the church from 1828 until his death Dec. 17, 1872, at the age of seventy-six, and its clerk for forty years,

*A biographical sketch of Dea. Choate was published in *The Congregational Quarterly*. Vol. xvii. No. 4.

the particular form of service for the church in which he took the greatest delight and to which he devoted his best energies was the management of this institution, the superintendence of which from his appointment to it in 1837, he held through a long life, and to which he imparted the peculiar character for which it has been so widely known, largely by the general exercise he introduced, in which he himself reviewed and commented upon the important points of the lessons statedly assigned. Into this informal instruction he entered with a genuine enthusiasm. So well did he know the avenues to the youthful mind and heart and with such tact could he address himself to those who were older, that his expositions of the word of God were "like apples of gold in pictures of silver," or "as nails fastened by the masters of assemblies." Discerning well that "the imagination is the grand organ by which the truth can make successful approaches to the mind," he would so picture a Bible scene, sketch one of its characters, or illumine whatever particular truth was under consideration, that his hearers could not fail to comprehend and to carry away a lasting impression.

This general exercise, however, was not confined to the lesson for the day, but had great variety given to it in many ways and thus became the distinguishing feature of the school, sustaining and deepening the interest of all who were connected with it, binding them together like members of one family and becoming a most effective means of religious training.

The Sabbath school has been always large in numbers; it has been noted for the system with which it has been conducted and its liberal gifts to benevolent objects; but its real excellence has lain in its remarkable power to mould the characters of those who have grown up under its influence. It has set upon them its impress like the seal upon wax.

One proof of this, which may be appropriately referred to here, is found in the significant fact that most if not all of those who have been actively engaged in these various forms of Christian work, which have peculiarly characterized the last seventy years, received their own religious training in this nursery of the church. Among them (in addition to those already mentioned) may be named Messrs. Uriah G. Spofford, John S. Burnham, Jeremiah Cogswell, Nathan Burnham, 3d, Moses Perkins and Robert W. Burnham, together with the present officers and other members of the church.

A full exhibition of the history and work of the School during its first fifty years has fortunately been preserved in the elaborate, complete and exceedingly interesting historical address delivered by Superintendent Choate at its semi centennial anniversary, which was celebrated by public exercises, Dec. 26, 1864.

While each of these three periods in the history of this church, over which we have cast our backward glance, is thus seen to have its peculiar characteristics and its special mission, while there is exhibited to us through the records of each era in turn the foundation work of the seventeenth century, the reconstructive and uplifting work of the eighteenth century and the Sabbath School and other Christian work of the laity in the nineteenth century, yet we can also see as we trace the thread of events, as we gather up and examine the various incidents falling under our notice along the pathway we have taken and picture to ourselves the differing scenes bright or dark, by passing through which this church has been cheered or chastened, that these periods are only successive stages,— the infancy, youth and maturity — of one and the same life, which "vital in every part cannot but by annihilating die," and which may never grow old, but by waiting upon the Lord may ever renew its strength.

And it is the underlying and unchanging, substantial qualities of this life, first and foremost the loving spirit of Jesus the Lord with which this church has ever been inspired, the strength of its faith and the truth of its creed attested by its fruitfulness in all good works, the scriptural simplicity of its church order and the purity and power of its pulpit, which have made it to so great a degree the conservative, elevating, purifying element in society, and which therefore demand on this commemoration-day the tribute of our deepest reverence and our warmest affection and gratitude.

This life of the church, however, really consists in the life of its individual members. And so it is the piety and devotion, the ability and learning of its ministers; it is the long line and the solid column of its laymen of vigorous minds, with their diversity of gifts but animated by the same spirit, rock-like in the solidity of their Christian principle, thrifty "as the trees of lignaloes which the Lord hath planted," flourishing and fruitful even in old age; it is the goodly company of saintly women, whose lives have been like an alabaster box of precious ointment, broken and poured out at the feet of their Divine Lord in consecration to His service, in their approving themselves in all things as servants of God, by pureness, by love unfeigned, by the armor of righteousness, and by the almsdeeds which they have done;— Yes, it is the dear fathers and mothers, your ancestors and mine, who wrought their very being into this church and brought us under its benign and blessed influences, before whose memories we rise up to-day in reverence and honor, and for whom, on this occasion, we have reason for giving our humble and most hearty thanks to Him who is the head over all things to the church.

Six generations of this host have already crossed the flood. Many of those with whom our own lives are linked by holiest ties and precious recollections have vanished out of our sight, though they still seem to hover about us, and we now and then instinctively turn to behold the faces and hear the voices of those we have so loved and revered; and with reference to them we must use the poet's words:

"Look where we may, the wide earth o'er,
Those lighted faces smile no more,
We tread the paths their feet have worn,
We sit beneath the orchard trees,
We hear, like them, the hum of bees
And rustle of the bearded corn;
Their written words we linger o'er,
But in the sun they cast no shade,
No voice is heard, no sign is made,
No step is on the conscious floor."

Yet, of all these faithful followers of a divine Master who came among men not to be ministered unto but to minister, of them all whose ambition was righteousness and Christian service, it may in truth be said that though they had none of that renown among men which has been compared to "a snowflake on hot water, a touch and it's vanished," for "the brighest names that earth can boast just glisten and are gone," still their works do follow them. Such characters of spiritual strength and beauty, as they were fashioned into, are and always will be a living force in the community, in themselves a benefaction to the world around them of substantial and permanent value.

Address on Rev. John Wise.

There seem to have been four classes among the early settlers of the Massachusetts Colony. There were first, those who paid for their passage and stood in the same relation as if original subscribers of £50 to the common stock; second, those contributing skill in art or trade, who received remunerative in money or land; third, those who exhausted their humble ability in paying a part of their expenses, agreeing to earn the rest here; and, fourth, those who came distinctly as indentured serving-men, who, in return, were held to labor for a term of years; having a claim the while for support from their masters. This last class was, possibly, more numerous than has been always understood. Thomas Dudley in his Letter to the Countess of Lincoln, of date 12-22 Mar. 1630*, says that when Winthrop's company arrived, in the summer before, they found the condition of those who had been sent over in the previous two years so straitened and grievous, that, lacking provisions, they were obliged to cancel the indentures of all who remained of *one hundred and eighty* such serving-men, although it had cost from £16 to £20 apiece to bring them over.

Such serving-men naturally came from humble homes, but many of them were worthy and faithful; and they, or their children, rose to respectability and usefulness in the commonwealth.

*Young's Chronicles of Mass. 311.

In Winthrop's Company was one George Alcock, who had married the sister of Thomas Hooker,* who was a physician and deacon; of whom John Eliot left on the Roxbury church-book the loving and creditable record, that:† "he lived in a good and godly sort, and dyed in the end of the 10th month ano. 1640, and left a good savor behind him; the Pore of the church much bewailing his losse." In the ten years of his New England life Dr. Alcock made two voyages to England, in the latter of which, probably,‡ he brought over, as an indentured attendant of the fourth class referred to, one Joseph Wise. Making his will a few days before his death, he inserted this clause:§ "to my servant Joseph Wise [I give] my young heifer, & the rest of his time from after mid-somer next." Joseph made so good use of his time, not to mention the heifer, that a little inside of five months [3–13 Dec. 1641] after the midsummer in question, he married Mary Thompson.‖ In the nearly three-and-forty years between that date and his death, 12–22 September 1684, thirteen children from his household were baptized in Roxbury, to wit:** Joseph, Jeremiah, Sarah, Mary, *John*, Henry, Bethia, Katharine, Benjamin, William, Benjamin (again), Abigail and Jeremiah (the second). John, third son and fifth child, was baptized 15–25 July 1652, just five months and eight days before the death of John Cotton. Thomas Hooker had been dead five years and a week; John Wilson was sixty-four; Charles Chauncy, sixty; Richard Mather, fifty-six; John Davenport, fifty-five; John Eliot, forty-eight; John Norton, forty-six; and Increase Mather, a lad of thirteen, had been already a year in Harvard College. It is this John Wise whom we are now to consider.

We are left to absolute conjecture, founded upon the simple

---

*Savage Gen. Dict. 1: 21.
†Report of Boston Record Commission. 1881. 76. ‡Savage. IV: 614.
§N. E. Hist. and Gen. Reg. 11: 104. ‖Savage IV: 614.
** Report Rec. Com. 1881: 116, 117, 118, 119, 121, 122, 123, 124, 125, 126, 135.

abstract probabilities of the case, for all idea of his childhood
and youth. "The child is father of the man," and therefore
the man prophesies the child; and, as it is matter of record*
that, in his adult years, this man "was of a majestic form, and
of great muscular strength and activity," I entertain no doubt
that he was a stout, sun-burned, hardy, vigorous, fun-loving
boy; and, as he started from the bottom round of the social
ladder, that he worked for his living, and got his pliant muscles well-strung and stalwart, by diligent and untrivial toil.
Whatever, in forest, field, farm-buildings or smithy, with ax,
plow, flail, hoe or hammer, his father did; that — beyond
question — John helped him do, growing hungrier, heavier
and tougher, day by day. I fancy he was one of those lads,
— some of us remember them :
—*quaeque ipse miserrima vidi,
et quorum pars magna fui.*
whom, in the good old days before farming was reduced to
riding in a gig with some kind of a plowing, mowing or reap-
ing machine in tow, it was safe to send off in advance with
the first scythe in an overlapping series of mowers; recognizing his abundant ability not merely to keep his own ancles
out of the way of the swinging blades of his pursuers, but to
lead them such a rush as to make them wiltingly willing now
and then to cry halt, wipe their brows, make music with their
whetstones, and pass the jug.

We shall never know through precisely what agencies, or
by precisely what influences, this young man awoke to the
consciousness that he had in him stuff of which something
better for his generation even than a good farmer, or a cunning
workman, might be made. I imagine that he caught from
the seraphic zeal of the good apostle to the Algonkins some
kindling of desire to make others happier and better, and that
that keen mind whose holy business it was to watch for signs
of the progress of the Gospel in so many savage breasts,

---

*Sprague's Annals, i: 189.

failed not to discern, and to stimulate, the beginnings of a higher life in the mind of a young parishioner so full of promise.

The "Free Schoole in Roxburie"—still in vigorous life, and at which my own son was fitted for Yale—had already been in existence near seven years when John Wise was born. On the 22 Nov.-2 Dec. after his birth,[†] "convenient benches with formes with tables, for the scholars to sit on and to write at, with a convenient seat for the school master, and a deske to put the Dictionary on, and shelves to lay up bookes," had been duly provided for it. Doubtless our lad got his beginnings at home. But that, when qualified to do so, he became at least an occasional occupant of one of these "convenient seats," is rendered almost certain by an ancient document in admirable chirography bearing date 25 Feb.-6 Mar., 1668-69[‡], in which it is agreed between the six feoffees and John Prudden that—for the sum of £25 a year, to be paid "three quarters in Indian Corn, or Peas, and ye other fourth-parte in Barley, all good and merchandable"—said Prudden shall keep the school, and "use his best skill & endeavor, both by precept & example, to instruct in all scholasticall, morall, & theologicall discipline, the children (soe far as they are, or shall be, capable)," of fifty-eight persons, "whose names are thereunder written—all ABCdarians excepted." On the list of these fifty-eight parents appears the name of John's father, "Joseph Wise."

From Thomas Mighill,[§] the last previous incumbent—born at Rowley, who had graduated at Harvard College in 1663, and was subsequently pastor at Milton, and South Scituate;—and John Prudden[‖]—son of Rev. Peter of Milford, Conn., who had graduated at Harvard in 1668, and afterward preached at Jamaica, L.I., Rye, Conn., and Newark, N.J., then relapsing

---

[*] Dillaway's Hist. Rox. Gram. School, etc. p. 7.
[†] Ibid. p. 26.
[‡] Ibid. frontispiece.
[§] Sibley's Har. Graduates, ii : 144. [‖] Ibid ii : 258.

into school-teaching once more, and sending out several eminent pupils — it is probable that the lad obtained his real training for his college course; which was, most likely, largely accomplished by what sporting men would call a spurt of eighteen months of vigorous endeavor last preceding entrance. Over and beyond the common English branches, this training consisted* in the acquirement of a sufficient knowledge of Latin to be able to read *ex tempore* Tully, or some equivalent classic, and "to make and speak true Latin in verse and prose;" with a sufficient knowledge of Greek to be able to "decline perfectly the paradigms of nouns and verbs" in that tongue. As the course of study, which from 1640 to 1654 had included but three years, was at the latter date lengthened to four,† and as Wise graduated in the class of 1673, he appears to have entered college in 1669, when he would be seventeen years old.

Harvard College, then founded about thirty years, and which had sent out near 200 graduates, at that time had visible existence on a spacious plain near the river, "a place very pleasant and accomodate,"‡ in a single wooden building originally comely without, but by this time sadly out of repair; having in it§ "a spacious Hall — where they daily met at Commons, Lectures, &c — and a large Library with some Bookes to it," having also chambers for lodging and closets for study, and "all other roomes of office necessary and convenient;" flanked on the one Hand by a modest Grammar School a little predating itself, taught by Master Elijah Corlett for nearly half a century,∥ and on the other by a small brick building then recently erected by the Society for the Propagation of the Gospel, for the encouragement and accomodation of Algonkin students.

* Laws, etc., Quincy's Hist. Har. Un. i: 515.
† The Harvard Book i: 33.
‡ N. Eng. First Fruits, 12. Sibley's Har. Grad. i: 7.
§ Ibid.
∥ Paige's Hist. Cambridge, p. 366.

There would be from twenty-five to thirty undergraduate scholars, with perhaps one third as many more who had taken their first degree and continued in residence, pursuing further study with a view to the second degree and a profession. Such were called "Sir" Smith, "Sir" Brown*—and so on—until they became Masters of Arts. The President was the only real officer. There were no professors.† Some of the "Sirs" acted as tutors; for which they received the munificent sum of £4 a year.‡ As the College was then a public institution it was subjected to the distinctions which pervaded the State, and soon after admission the members of the Freshman Class were "placed" according to the social rank of their families, and thenceforth at the table, at worship, in recitation and everywhere, were required to conform to the order fixed. The best rooms, and best seats, and even the first helpings at the table, thus belonged to the sons of the "first families;" so that we may be sure that John Wise was frequently and effectually reminded that his father was a nobody; and, very likely, that flame of his democracy which forty years later burst into a scorching and consuming blaze, began here, and now, to kindle and smolder. Furthermore there were sharp distinctions of rank between classes, as well; the lower being the fag and drudge of the upper, not merely, but the Freshman being obliged to take off his hat not only to the President and Tutors, but also if one of the upper classes happened to come into the College yard. In either case said Freshman was obliged to remain uncovered until the more respectable party entered the building and disappeared from view.§ Nor was discipline by any means an empty word. No student without special parental permission founded upon a physician's certificate—and "then in a sober and private manner"—could use tobacco;‖ nor could he "buy, sell, or exchange

* Sibley. i: 17.
† Harv'd. Book. i: 30.   ‡ Ibid.   § Ibid. 28.
‖ By J. Danker's account of his visit in 1680, there had been much backsliding as to this. Mem. Long Isld. Hist. Soc. i: 384.

anything to the value of six-pence, without the allowance of his parents, guardians, or Tutors;" nor frequent the company of men of "ungirt and dissolute life;" while, if under age [*nisi adultus*] after twice admonition, any who perversely or negligently transgressed any law of God, or of the college, became liable to a whipping in the Hall openly — the culprit kneeling down, and the President opening and closing the "exercise" with prayer.* In a smaller and quiet way, the Tutors thrashed the boys at discretion.† Plum cake, for some reason which does not appear, was especially disreputable, and a few years later its use imperiled one's degree.‡ Fines abounded and money was scarce. College bills were apt to be paid in farm-products, garden "sauce," and merchandise.

I regret to say that in September of his Senior Year, our friend was caught in a scrape which proved that College human nature was at that time much as it has usually averaged. Edward Pelham — the most "respectable" man in his class, — it seems, had humbugged a young son of Urian Oakes into shooting a turkey belonging to some neighbor, which, turkey, being surreptitiously cooked by one Sam Gibson, was eaten on the night following by the said Pelham, *John Wise*, and one Jonathan Russell, then a Sophomore.§ The innkeeper Gibson — although he and his wife insisted they had no idea that the turkey was stolen — was admonished and fined forty shillings, and committed until it was paid. What was done to the offending students is not so clear from the record, as — what was done with the turkey!

It was distinctly avowed, "that Christ lay in the bottom, as the only foundation of all sound knowledge and Learning;" and secret prayer, and reading scripture twice daily, were

*Laws, etc. Quincy's Hist. Harv. Univ. i: 516; S. Sewall's Diary. 5 Mass. Hist. Coll. v: 4.
† Quincy, i: 189.
‡ Harvard Book, i: 40.
§ Sibley, ii: 416.
  Rules, etc., Sibley, i: 11, 12.

especially enjoined. Profaneness and neglect of worship were forbidden, and diligence in every duty demanded. At seven o'clock in the morning and at five o'clock in the afternoon, each student was required to attend prayers in his Tutor's chamber, and to give report of his own private reading of the Word.

Scholarship was clearly as much better than now in some respects, as it was worse in others. No English was allowed to be spoken on any occasion*—the sole exception being now and then a public declamation in the vernacular. No scholar could get his first degree who was not able, at sight, to translate the sacred Hebrew and Greek—flavored with Chaldee and Syriac†—into Latin, and "resolve them logically." And none could get his second, who did not satisfy the Overseers of his due proficiency also in Logic, Natural and Moral Philosophy, Arithmetic, Geometry, Astronomy, History, Botany and Rhetoric.‡

Wise happened upon Cambridge in changeful times. The venerable Chauncy was President when he entered, but died in his Junior year; so that he graduated during the obscurely sad and brief term of Leonard Hoar, and took his second degree under the acting presidency of Urian Oakes. Joseph Browne, who died at 32 just as he was to be settled over the Charlestown Church, John Richardson who afterward spent one-and-twenty years as teacher of the Church in Newbury; and possibly Daniel Gookin, who expended years of labor upon the Indians near Sherborne, were his Tutors.§ There were but four members of his class, viz.: Edward Pelham, George Alcock, Samuel Angier, and John Wise. Though a common, it was not the universal custom with these "Sir" Knights of learning who had just become Bachelors of Arts, and were looking forward to a second degree from the College, to

---

* Laws, etc., Quincy, I: 517.
† Ibid. (18). ‡ Ibid. (19), and I: 191.
§ Sibley, I: 207, 210, 277.

remain in residence, and pursue three further years of study in Cambridge. And—possibly because he was twenty-one, possibly because he was poor, possibly because he had common sense enough to know that *he* could do better elsewhere, and still more possibly because he was full-grown, handsome, liked people in general and was well-liked of them—John Wise chose other places for these years. As to what path precisely, and what inducements, he followed, we lack evidence; but in a few months we hear of him as preaching and being so well in Bradford, Conn., that they wanted him to settle against his will. Certain it is that when Philip's War was raging, in 1675, he was there, for it is on the Connecticut Records* that, 14–24 Jan. 1675–6, the Council of that Colony "appoynted Mr. Wise of Bradford, to goe forthe minister to our army, and accordingly wrote a letter to him to prepare and goe forthe with the sea-side forces to New London, there to meet with Major Treate, &c;" and we further find from a letter of Major Palmes,† dated at New London twelve days later, that our young friend accepted that chaplaincy, and had then just marched with the troops into the Narragansett country. We next hear of him as back at Cambridge at Commencement, 5–15 July, of that same year, where he delivered one of the two Master's Orations, affirmatively discussing the thesis, *An impossibile sit mandatum fuisse ab aeterno.‡*

About this time a minister was wanted at Hatfield, where Rev. Hope Atherton, of the class of 1665 at Cambridge, had been settled in 1671, but was now demented and dying in consequence of exposure and being lost in the woods in the Indian war;‡ and Wise took his place and preached there some two years after his death, but was unwilling to settle, and came back to Roxbury, where—I do not say this was

---

*Col. Rec. of Conn. 1675 1677. 399.
†Ibid. 402.
‡Sibley, ii. 193.

why he came back — 5-15 Dec. 1678, he married Abigail Gardner.*

Our next bit of news concerning him brings him hither. Although we had not here in Massachusetts, so long ago as in the latter quarter of the 17th century, arrived at a Governor who directed the ministers what not to preach about on Fast Day; we had an "honorable General Court" which made it a part of its concern that vacant churches should secure pastors which enjoyed its confidence.

I need not repeat to your well-instructed ears the story of the three years of endeavor which proved needful to overcome the reluctance of the town and the first church in Ipswich to the establishment of a church here, on the one hand; and to provide a candidate for the new pulpit, whom the Court should esteem able, pious, orthodox and Congregational, on the other. Suffice it to say that by 22 May-1 June, 1680, the "Jebacco" company of believers presented to the Committee of the Court "Mr. John Wise, as a person upon whom they have unanimously agreed upon for their minister."†

The Committee liked him, and the Court‡ did "allow & accept thereof." How long he had been here, or how much he had preached to the people, does not appear, but he soon came among them to gladden them for the rest of his days.

It would be surplusage — after the historical review which you have already heard, and in the face of that admirable volume§ by one of your former pastors, which in such a fit and pleasing manner enshrines your annals, and which I trust is in nearly all your houses — were I to dwell upon the details of the service here of your distinguished first pastor. I may only glance at it, as, in three departments, it magnificently illustrates the best qualities of the New England ministry of a past age, while, at the same time, in so doing manifesting the

---

* Savage. iv : 614.
† Mass. Col. Rec. v : 285.   ‡ Ibid. 286.
§ History of the Town of Essex, etc., by Rev. R. Crowell. D.D., 1868.

real greatness of the man himself. I refer particularly to the relation of the old-time pastor among us — always nearly the best-educated man, often almost the only well educated man, in town; the man of broad discretion, far sight and large hope, as well as profound religious faith — to civil and social, as well as ecclesiastical affairs.

It was inevitable that, in their civil matters, the masses of the people in their first century here should look very much toward the ministers for guidance as to public affairs. It was on all hands conceded that religious considerations largely led to the emigration; what, therefore, so natural as that the ministers of religion should be looked to to water the young tree in its new soil. It was very far from priest-craft, or even assumption, or ambition, in the clergy which led to their being largely consulted in the Massachusetts Colony in its earlier days by the magistrates. Not only were the pastors of these flocks in the wilderness, by the high range of their studies presumed to be more familiar than other men with political ethics and the science of jurisprudence, but the fact that they were experts in self-government in the church, suggested that they might easily contribute valuable aid toward those Colonial transactions which from the beginning were largely marked by self-government in the State. Moreover the influence which came westward over the sea during the times of the Commonwealth at home, could not fail on the one hand to set the people to asking, and on the other to prompt their spiritual teachers toward contributing, counsel — and sometimes something more — to the affairs of the town, and the Colony. And when unexpected, and sometimes startling, problems suddenly demanded decision, it was of all things most natural that the freemen should look toward the Elders for suggestion.

Mr. Wise was always ready to accept his full measure of responsibility and toil for the State. His brief service with the troops from Connecticut in Philip's war was followed by a much more responsible and important service of the like description, when, in 1690, the Legislature of Massachusetts sent him as chaplain to that ill-judged, ill-planned, ill-managed, ill-fated and in-glorious expedition of Sir William Phips for the conquest of Canada. Mr. Wise seems, indeed to have been about the only man who brought home any increase of renown; but it is clear that beyond the pious discharge of the special duties of his sacred office, he greatly distinguished himself by "his Heroick Spirit, and Martial Skill and Wisdom," and it is certain that more than forty years after the event, and more than ten years after he himself was dead, his family received from the State substantial proof of the honor in which his memory was held in consequence.*

Much more of moral, and perhaps quite as much of physical, courage was however demanded by the action which, in 1687, he took in resistance to what he believed to be civil tyranny. The exasperating — yet possibly over-hated — Sir Edmund Andros had been for more than two years Governor of a New England consolidated from the separate Colonies, by what the colonists felt to be the unwarrantable abrogation of the Charters, under which for almost two generations they had lived in peace and prosperity, and upon whose validity not only their public legislation, but all their private property titles, depended. If the new measures were sustained, it was literally true that there was not an acre of land between the Penobscot and the Hudson, which — however guarded by legal papers — had not thus reverted to King James the Second; and which, with all its belongings, could not be sold or given away — in the face of those who had bought, paid, sweat and bled for it — to whomsoever he liked. There was a new flag and a new seal, and new ways altogether. Andros seemed to our fathers of that day to be purely a despot; and this new New England simply his despotism. As to taxation he was empowered — with the assent of his

---

*Sibley, ii: 132.

compliant Council—to impose such taxes as he pleased, and send them down to the towns to be by them assessed, collected and paid. It became his pleasure thus to impose a tax of a penny on the pound—say $4.00 on the thousand. A little after the middle of August 1687 an order came to this town, that such a tax be levied and collected here.

William Hubbard—the well-known historian—was pastor of the First Church, and lacked but little of his three-score years and ten. Perhaps for this reason; perhaps on account of his "singular Modesty;"* possibly because of some occult personal tie indicated by the fact that Andros selected him to preside at the next Commencement of Harvard College—where he had the taste, in his oration, to compare Sir William to Jason fetching the Golden Fleece;†—we do not hear of him as taking an active part in the commotion which followed. But we do hear of John Wise—then five-and-thirty; at which age a self-poised man is apt to think reasonably well of himself, and an active, effervescent man to feel equal to almost any contract social or civil. Mr. Wise, with two of his parishioners went over to Ipswich proper on Monday 22 Aug.–1 Sept. 1687—doubtless the thing had been talked over between meetings the day before—to the house of Mr. John Appleton, where several principal inhabitants of the town were quietly assembled, in what we should call a caucus. They reached the deliberate conclusion that "it was not the Town's duty any way to assist that ill method of raising money, without a General Assembly, which was apparently intended by Sir Edmund and his Council."‡ And the next day in town-meeting John Wise made a speech in which he said that they had a good God, and a good king, and would do well to trust in them, stand to their privileges as Englishmen, and quietly refuse to cooperate in a procedure which "doth infringe their

---

* John Dunton, Life and Errors, etc. cited in Sibley, i : 58.
† Sewall, Diary. 5 Mass. Hist. Coll. v : 219.
‡ Sibley, ii : 430.

Liberty;"* and the town voted — without a single negative — against compliance with the Governor's order.

For this, Mr. Wise, as ringleader, with five others, was speedily arrested and lodged in Boston jail "for contempt and high misdemeanour;"† was refused a *habeas corpus* by Chief Justice Dudley; was tried at Oyer and Terminer, and found guilty. Mr. Wise was "suspended from the Ministerial Function" fined £50 and costs, and required to give "a‡ thousand pound bond for the good behavior one year," while his companions were also fined and disqualified from office.

But "the whirligig of time" was not long in bringing "in his revenges." Before twenty months had passed, Andros — anticipating the scheme of a great traitor of later date — was trying to escape in women's clothes from the jail on Castle Island,§ and Wise was back in Boston as one of the Ipswich members of the Convention which was reestablishing the old government; and under the new flag of William and Mary, sued Chief Justice Dudley for having denied him the *habeas corpus*; with the result, it is stated, of recovering damages.∥

These incidents, with what they suggest, will be further illustrated when we come to glance at Mr. Wise's Congregational teachings; which moved men more mightily toward our present republicanism than those of any one of his cotemporaries, and can leave us in no doubt that, in this department of civil influence, few men — if any man — of his day excelled your Chebacco pastor.

There are, moreover, good words to be spoken of him in the matter of a more purely social inspiration. Over and above all those ceaseless and countless promptings toward daily improvement of some sort, which an educated leader of the community whom all love and respect, and whose great powers are matter at once of common admiration and

* Ibid.
† Crowell's Hist. Essex. p. 102.
‡ Sibley, ii : 132.
§ Palfrey, Hist. N. Eng. iii : 583.   ∥ Crowell, 103.

enjoyment, is giving forth as unconsciously as the climbing sun is banishing the night-shadows; Mr. Wise wrote his name upon the history of the last quarter of the 17th and the first quarter of the 18th century, in connection with some definite endeavors to make men happier as well as better.

In Feb. 1696-7* there was a movement on the part of certain residents of his vicinity to emigrate to South Carolina, and settle on the Ashley river, near a company already gone from Dorchester; and Mr. Wise placed in the hands of "Wm. Haskel, Sen., Purser for the Company of Subscribers for ye voiage," certain admirable "Instructions for Emigrants from Essex County, Mass. who Intend to Remove themselves and families into South Carolina."

In that wave of darkness which swept over New England in the last decade of the 17th century, when the superstition which still shrouded the old country drifted across the Atlantic and settled down into the night of the witchcraft delusion over the new, John Wise was one of the very small number of men having sagacity enough, boldness enough, and firmness enough, in the face of whatsoever danger, to resist the sweeping fanaticism. Mr. Upham—who seldom went out of his way to compliment men of a sterner faith than his own—in his *History of the Salem Witchcraft*—† says: "Mr. Wise was a learned, able, and enlightened man. He had a free spirit, and was perhaps the only minister in the neighborhood or country, who was discerning enough to see the erroneousness of the proceedings from the beginning." He risked his own life to save, if possible, his neighbor John Procter, and others, from their terrible fate. And, 8-19 July 1703, we find him conspicuously signing an "Address" to the General Court, which declared:‡ "there is great reason to fear that innocent persons suffered, and that God may have a controversy with the land upon that account," and earnestly begging

* Sibley, ii: 433.
† Salem Witchcraft, etc. ii: 304.
‡ Ibid. 477.

at least for the tardy justice involved in declaring null and void the attainders resting upon the heirs of those unfortunate victims—a prayer after more than seven years of further delay at last tardily granted.*

Sometimes radicals grow conservative, if not timid, as they advance in life, but it evidences the genuineness of this man's independence of thought and action, that when he was nearing his three-score years and ten, he took part in the exciting controversy which then raged in the churches as to singing by note, and wrote to Thomas Symmes† his judgement: "That when there were a sufficient number in a Congregation to carry away a Tune Roundly, it was proper to introduce that Tune." So when, in 1721, almost all the physicians, except Dr. Zabdiel Boylston, were bitterly opposing the new practice of inoculation for the small-pox which Cotton Mather was trying to introduce,‡ and the vulgar rage so flamed against it that the rabble tried to hang Dr. Boylston, and blow up Cotton Mather's house; your Chebacco pastor took up the cudgels in favor of his life-long opponent and his novel doctrine, and was among the first to approve, and commend to practice, the simple and effectual, if then startling, remedy.

You will agree with me that all these were great features of humanity, and that only of a great and grand man could they have been true. But I seem to myself only just now to approach the real greatness of John Wise, as I ask you, in the last place, to consider his character in its relation to the Church Polity under which he lived.

The first man, of whom we have certain knowledge, after the semi-Reformation under Henry VIII., to rediscover the original Congregationalism, was Robert Browne.§ But—as all deep thinkers have—he had a philosophy of his own by which he explained the outward facts. As he looked at it, all

---

* Sibley. ii : 433.
† T. Symmes. Utile Dulci. etc. 55.
‡ Memorial History of Boston. etc. 537 ; Crowell. 131.
§ See as to Browne and his views, etc. Cong. of last 300 years. etc. 98-110.

church power resides in Christ; yet Christ reveals His will to, and works in, all believers. So that the Saviour's absolute monarchy, reaching expression through all faithful persons equally as His vicegerents, becomes practically indistinguishable from a pure democracy; because to outward eye there can be no difference between a government of the people exercised because each has inborn inherent right to rule, and one exercised because each acts as by proxy, and substitutionally, as the channel of the power of another. With this central principle Browne held other related ones, some of which —particularly the constant duty of mutual criticism—proved wholly impracticable, and inapplicable to the unculture of those humble rustics whom, mainly, he gathered around him. Mutual criticism with them soon degenerated into scolding, impertinent scrutiny, crimination and recrimination, until the little church of poor and ignorant people, unfit for responsibilities for which they had never enjoyed needful preparation, went to pieces in Middelberg, in confusion and anarchy.

The next Apostle of early modern Congregationalism, Henry Barrowe, seems to have accepted Browne's system in the main, but sought to avoid what had proved fatal to the church in Zeland, by arranging that the management be in the hands of the few wisest and best members; concerning whom the mass of the church should have the two liberties: (1) to elect; (2) ever after to obey them. This, of course, was Presbyterio-Congregationalism; Presbyterian in its Eldership, Congregational in its local church and the right and duty of that church to manage its own affairs without control from without. This scheme was Barrowism in distinction from Brownism. The Amsterdam and Leyden Separatists were Barrowists, although John Robinson, by having but a single Ruling Elder, and by using large conference with the membership always before action, steered his ship much nearer the Congregational, than the Presbyterian side of the channel.

New England Congregationalism began as Barrowism. The

Presbyterians had almost no fault to find with it, and expressly declared it "well sound,"* had it but "given a *little* more power to Synods." It was essentially Genevan in its College of Elders, (of which the Pastor was chief) inside the local congregation; essentially Brownistic outside of it. And no one then regarded Democracy as a good, or even tolerable, thing in church or state.

Time passed. Practice began to develop the fact that the essentials of an irrepressible conflict were inborn and inbred in this hybrid system. It was impossible to explain and enforce the right of every church-member to share in the government of the body, without demonstrating the absurdity of the claim that all church-members must submit to be governed by the Elders; and, on the other hand, it was even more impossible to establish the right of the Elders, at least to negative every church act, without emptying the claim of the people to rule, of all possible value. As it proved, moreover, very difficult to obtain in each of the little scattered churches of those days five or six men having sense and culture enough to discharge acceptably the duties of Ruling Elders; that office — as to which, to tell the truth, the regnant good sense of New England was never hearty — fell into disuse. This left the Pastor sole representative of the Eldership, and crowned him singly with the right, if not to govern the church, at least to prevent it from governing itself, by negativing every church act which he might not approve.

The Half-way Covenant, with its influx of semi-members, and their diluting effect upon the average both of Orthodoxy of faith and spirituality of life, had at length reduced the churches to a condition of alarming depression. Some laid the blame upon the fact that Councils could only advise, and never command or control. Others thought the difficulty was in the well-nigh complete disuse of Ruling Elders. And, in 1700, Increase Mather lifted up his voice in anguish to

---

* Rutherford, Ratio, etc. 7.

warn all parties:* "if this begun Apostasy should proceed as fast the next thirty years as it has done these last, surely it will come to that in New England (except the Gospel it self depart with the Order of it) that the most Conscientious People therein, will think themselves concerned to gather Churches out of Churches."

But what was to be done? He, and others like him, who were sagacious in their way, had their answer. And, in 1705, the Boston Association of ministers adopted and sent forth "Certain Proposals," in their judgment eminently adapted to heal the hurt of the daughter of God's people, by going back into the Egypt of "strong" governments for help. A system of Associations of ministers was to have charge of all Church affairs. There were to be Standing Councils to determine all doubtful matters. No Minister uncommended by such an Association was to enter a vacant pulpit. And so on.†

This scheme included some good points. But, in the main, it was founded on the false and foolish notion that an attenuated, decrepid and moribund Congregationalism could be reanimated, and rejuvenated, by a heroic dose of Presbyterianism.

It was in the Autumn of 1705 that this Pamphlet of Proposals made its way to Chebacco. John Wise read it and laughed at it. And for three or four years he anticipated concerning it that policy which Cotton Mather twenty years later boasted that he had exercised with regard to Mr. Wise's own book, namely that of "generoso silentio, et pio contemptu."‡ But when, in 1708, the Connecticut Colony convoked the Saybrook Synod, and followed its lead into Consociationism as the established religion, Chebacco was stirred. The impossible seemed in danger of happening, and lest the

* Order of the Gospel, etc. 11.
† See Proposals etc., as reprinted by J. Wise, in his Churches Quarrel espoused.
‡ Ratio Dis. etc. 18.

churches of the Bay be seduced into a like infidelity to their own first principles, John Wise took up his pen, and put his laugh and the philosophy of it into a dense, learned, logical and tremendously caustic 16mo. pamphlet of one hundred and fifty pages, which was printed in 1710. He pitched in to the "Proposals" without pity, and — in a style unique for those days, at once of singular directness, force, and brilliancy — he showed that the proposition really made was that the churches surrender their God-given rights for the sake of a new polity, which seemed to be "a Conjunction of almost all the Church Governments in the World, & the least part is Congregational.* Indeed at the first cast of the Eye, the scheme seems to be the Spectre or Ghost of Presbyterianism, or the Government of the Church by Classes; yet if I don't mistake, in Intention there is something considerable of Prelacy in it . . . . something which smells very strong of the Infallible chair." . . . . so† strong of the Pope's Cooks and kitchen, where his Broths and Restoratives are prepared, that they are enough to strangle a Free-born Englishman, and much more those Churches, that have lived in such a clear Air, and under such enlargements so long a time." Lest any should think he was disproportioning the severity of his attack to the size of the enemy, he said:‡ "though it be but a Calf now, yet in time it may grow (being of a thirsty Nature) to become a sturdy Ox, that will know no *Whoa*, and it may be past the Churches skill then to subdue it." Perhaps the most scorching passage is one of his closing paragraphs in which referring to the anonymous character of the pamphlet — which, in deference to the taste of the time, merely announced itself as done by an Association "at B——" 5 November 1705 — he said: "where the Place was, or the Persons who were present in this Randezvouze, shall never be told by me, unless it be Extorted by the

---

* Churches Quarrels Espoused, etc. p. 38.
† Ibid. 108. ‡ Ibid. 81.

Rack. And tho' I have endeavored with freedom of Argument to subvert the Error, I will never stain their Personal Glory, by repeating or calling over the Muster Roll. Therefore, as Noah's Sons cast a Garment upon their Fathers Nakedness, so (leaving them in the Crowd) their Names (for me) shall repose under a Mantle of honourable pity and forgetfulness."*

Seven years later, when Mr. Wise was sixty-five, he published a formal treatise—this time a tome of only 105 pages—entitled a *Vindication of the Government of New England Churches*. He took the ground that democracy must be the best government for the Church, because it is the best government for the State. At a day when the idea was novel and unpopular, he avowed his conviction that the only rule thoroughly suited to man's nature, is one founded on the fundamental principle of human equality of rights. He was the first logical and clear-headed American democrat. Half a century before Thomas Jefferson, with irresistible logic and almost unmatched magnificence of style, he laid down the everlasting principles of democracy for both civil and ecclesiastical affairs. He did this so well that when more than half a century after, in 1772, the great work of the American revolution was in hand, two successive reprints in a single twelvemonth of his arguments demonstrated of how much value his writings seemed to those patriots who were seeking to achieve our national independence, and establish upon a firm basis in the convictions of intelligent men, our government—of the people, by the people, and for the people. Prof. Moses Coit Tyler in his *History of American Literature* cites from Mr. Wise this passage:† "The End of all good Government is to Cultivate Humanity and promote the Happiness of all, and the good of every Man in all his Rights, his Life, Liberty, Estate, Honour, etc., without injury or abuse done to any;" and says:‡ "No wonder that the writer of that sentence was

* Ibid. 115.   † Vindication, etc., 61.   ‡ Hist. Amer. Lit. ii: 116.

called up from his grave, by the men who were getting ready for the Declaration of Independence!" And I may quote here the same brilliant historian's general tribute to him whom we commemorate. He says:[*] "upon the whole, no other American author of the Colonial time is the equal of John Wise in the union of great breadth and power of thought with great splendor of style; and he stands almost alone among our early writers for the blending of a racy and dainty humor with impassioned earnestness."

That these two tremendous pamphlets left their mark upon our Congregationalism, need not be told in detail. They were surcharged with the electricity of original and energetic thought to that degree that some who were hit, felt almost as if their author had "shot out lightnings to discomfit them." And as thunder and lightening purify the air, these two little bolts clarified our whole atmosphere. The pregnant good sense which was in them not only prepared the way, but led the march, by which what was bad of Barrowism was left behind, and what was good of Brownism was recovered, until the reasonable and justly balanced self-government of that polity under which we now live, was perfected. So that to him who asks for some monument which shall illustrate and demonstrate the ecclesiastical influence of this man upon his own time, and upon all times—pointing to four thousand sensibly democratic Congregational Churches between the Aroostook and the Golden Gate, we may say of John Wise in those fit words which Mylne, architect of Blackfriars, inscribed over the entrance of the choir of St. Paul's Cathedral in London, to the memory of Christopher Wren, its builder: "*Si monumentum requiris, circumspice.*"

I wrote the other day to my friend Hon. J. Hammond Trumbull—the greatest, and (I may say) only, living authority upon the Algonkin tongue—asking for the exact sense of this word *Chebacco*. I could not help noting a singular appro-

[*] Ibid. 114.

priateness revealed by his reply. He says he regards it as meaning, literally, "the greatest pond, or principal source, of some stream." Was it not a fit thing that your first *Chebacco* pastor should be the principal source of the great river of that democratic polity which now gladdens so largely our land?

It is one hundred and fifty-eight years four months and three days, since, on Thursday, 8-19 April 1725, in his own house, on the spot where the mansion of the late Mr. John Mears now stands, John Wise — who had reached the ripe age of two-and-seventy years, seven months, and twenty-three days — lay a dying. To John White, of Gloucester, he had said in the beginning of his sickness:* "I have been a man of contention, but the state of the churches made it necessary. Upon the most serious review I can say *I have fought a good Fight*; and I have comfort in reflecting upon the same: I am conscious to myself that I have acted sincerely." Happy, my brethren, will it be for you, and for me — since we too have fallen upon times that sometimes are troublous — if we may approach our last hours with a like humble conviction!

And now, when his time is fully come, he expresses his deep sense of nothingness and unworthiness, and of his need of the Divine compassion, and with his last breath invokes upon himself, his widow and seven children, and his beloved church and people to the latest generation, the dear grace of God in Christ.

Then the pale and attenuated, but still majestic, form rests. The sweet light that beamed in winsome gentleness, or flashed in kindly, if withering, sarcasm, or frowned in deserved rebuke, from under the eye-brows, is eclipsed forever. And the voice that for almost two-and-forty years had led as well as taught in all good ways, and cheered as well as chid this people toward all good works, is heard no more at all.

With a kind of sacred awe — as if there were presumption in it — they prepare the body for its last repose, and lay it in

* J. White: The Gospel Treasure in Earthen Vessels, etc., 41.

the best room. Through the open windows come in the twitterings of the early spring birds praising God in the budding branches; and the sod which they lift as they dig his grave — larger and longer than is their wont — is green with returning life, and has in it the sweet prophecy of reviving after the winter of death, breathed by the faint odor of a few first violets.

On Sunday* a congregation from far and near crowds the meeting-house — the *new* meeting-house, which never resounded with his most imperial eloquence, but in which the last seven years of his ripest ministry had been exercised — and John White preaches his funeral sermon, declining to attempt properly to characterize the dead, for, said he:† "he who would do it to the life, must have his eloquence."

The next day he was "decently Buried amidst the Honors & Lamentations of his Distressed Friends, and of his Loving and Generous Flock, and at their Expense,"‡ and that he might sleep surrounded by those to whom his life had been given, his grave was ordered to be near the center of the burial-ground. And as they took their last look of his face and stalwart form how many of the old men turned away with moist eyes to say to each other in Shakespeare's thought — though not, consciously to themselves, in Shakespeare's words:

> He was a man, take him for all in all,
> We shall not look upon his like again.

And if the Spring sun shone warm and pleasant, no doubt many of them lingered a while, and sat down in little groups to chat pleasant things of the dead. One tells again the story§ of the strong man of Andover — as yet unwhipt of all — who took the trouble to ride over to Chebacco to try his muscles upon the parson; and how the good-humored parson, nothing loath, consented to the trial, and concluded a vic-

---

* Gospel Treasure, etc. preached 11 Apr. etc. Title page.
† Ibid. 41. ‡ Sibley ii: 438.
§ Felt. Hist. Ipswich, Essex and Hamilton. p. 259.

torious wrestling bout by gently flirting his overgrown antagonist over the fence into the street; and how the astonished stranger accepted the situation in the mild suggestion that if Mr. Wise would kindly toss his horse over after him, he would depart satisfied and in peace! And another says: "Well the parson could wrestle in prayer, too," and goes on to recall how, some years before, a pirate cruiser on the coast had kidnapped a boat's crew of Chebacco boys; and how, in his next Sunday morning's supplication Mr. Wise had remembered the poor fellows, and had said: * "Great God! if there be no other way for their deliverance, stengthen them to rise and butcher their enemies;" and how, in very deed, the boys came back that same week safe and sound, with the statement, that, on Sunday, seizing, on a sudden impulse, a favorable opportunity, they had sprung upon their captors and taken the vessel.

They all well agree that he was great, and that he was good —the best kind of good: singularly gentle for so strong a man.

Here, my friends, I think we have essentially his character in his name. He was *John*, and he was *Wise*; and so he was JOHN WISE!

Verily, with rare truth, it was chiseled on his tomb-stone:

FOR TALENTS, PIETY AND LEARNING, HE SHONE
AS A STAR OF THE FIRST MAGNITUDE.

Prof. Park's Prayer.

AT THE GRAVE OF REV. JOHN WISE.

This prayer was taken down in full by the Stenographer of the Congregationalist and printed in that paper, Aug. 30, 1883.

O Lord, our God, Thou art our God, and Thou wast the God of our fathers. We thank Thee for all of which we have now been reminded of

* Ibid.

Thy doings among the fathers of this parish and this town. We thank Thee for the great men whom Thou hast here raised up for the promotion of Thy cause throughout our land. We thank Thee for the good men who have served Thee faithfully in the world, and then have been gathered into this place; this garden of the Lord.

We thank Thee that we are allowed to stand near the venerable dust of him who has been laid in this spot. We thank Thee for all which we have heard this day of his great works, and his humble spirit. We praise and bless Thy name, O Lord, that Thou didst endue him with an excellent understanding, and a capacious memory, and a brilliant imagination; that Thou didst see fit to give unto him stores of learning and wealth of knowledge far beyond the time in which he lived; that Thou didst see fit to give him a clear insight into the nature of his fellow-men, and a clear foresight of that history which was to be enacted after he had gone from the earth. We thank Thee for all his bold thoughts, and his vigorous words; for the influence which he has exerted on the churches in this Commonwealth, and on the churches which are now springing up in remote parts of our land — in regions which were unknown and unnamed while he was upon the earth. We thank Thee that the seed which he sowed on the borders of this Eastern sea is springing up and bearing fruit along the shores of the Western sea, and throughout the length and breadth of this land — thirty, and sixty, and an hundred fold. We thank Thee that the principles which he elucidated have been laid at the basis of our national structure. We thank Thee that our government, in so great a degree, has been fashioned according to those wise rules which he proposed. We thank Thee that his influence in church and in State has been continued, even to the present time. We pray, O Lord, that it may be prolonged through generations yet to come; that the light which shone from his humble dwelling may still continue to shine upon the churches and the States of our Union. Wilt Thou say unto the sun, "Go not down," and to the moon, "Depart not from the valley of Ajalon!" May this light be continued, and may more and more rejoice in it.

We thank Thee, O God, that Thou hast revealed unto us that those who serve Thee faithfully shall be crowned with glory and honor and immortality; that the righteous shall be held in everlasting remembrance. We rejoice that Thou dost remember Thy covenant with Abraham, and dost bless the children, and children's children, even unto remote generations of them that serve Thee and keep Thy commandments. Wilt Thou grant that all who have listened to the words spoken this day may receive some new impulse to duty. Particularly may all the members of this parish and this church — calling to mind that here has been the fountain from which have issued streams that have made glad this land, and that Thou hast distinguished them, O Lord, above so many of their fellowmen — all feel their obligation to live a new life, devoted unto the God of Abraham and of Isaac and of Jacob, the God of our fathers, who led our fathers through the wilderness, and brought them out into a safe place; and grant, O Lord, that we who are now assembled may learn some new lesson of Thy providence here, as we stand in this garden, where so many fathers and mothers have wept for their children, because their children were not; where so many brothers and sisters have come with tears and gone out with sobs, because they should see the face of their loved ones no more. We thank Thee that we are permitted to stand on this ground, where so many prayers have been offered by godly men and godly women who have visited this venerable grave; and, O Lord, we pray Thee that the prayers which have been offered in this home of the dead may be answered even now, and may richest blessings come down upon us, because Thy weeping and wailing children have looked up to Thee from this place, and supplicated Thy blessing. May we form such resolutions as we should form if the dead in Christ should rise and now admonish us of our duty; such resolutions as we should form if the blessed departed ones should come down and encircle us as a great cloud of witnesses, beckoning us onward to a higher life and a nobler duty.

Oh grant that we may feel at this time our own nothingness, and our dependence on Jesus Christ. May we feel the infinite disparity there is between Thee and us. Thine is the sea, for Thou didst make it. The strength of the hills is Thine also, and of old didst Thou lay the foundations of the earth; and the heavens are the work of Thy hands. They shall perish, but Thou remainest; they shall all wax old as doth a garment, and as a vesture shalt Thou fold them up, and they shall be changed; but Thou art the same, and Thy years shall not fail. We are like the flower that in the morning flourisheth, and in the evening is cut down and withereth. Let us remember how frail we are. Our fathers, where are they? — and the prophets, do they live forever? We are strangers and sojourners before Thee, as were all our fathers. But we would walk as they walked, near unto God; and as Thy servant, around whose grave we stand, looked unto Jesus as the author and finisher of his faith, so may we all be prepared to die as he died, with reliance on Him who shed His blood for us; and grant, O Lord, at the great day when the trumpet shall sound and the dead shall be raised, that we may rise to immortal life; that this corruptible may put on incorruption, and this mortal put on immortality; and that we may be forever with the Lord. And may it be declared of us, when we are laid to rest, as of the venerable father near whose remains we stand, "Blessed are the dead which die in the Lord from henceforth; yea, saith the Spirit, that they may rest from their labors, and their works do follow them." And may each of us be able to say at the last, "I have fought a good fight; I have finished my course, I have kept the faith." And through the grace of Jesus Christ our Lord, shall be rendered unto Thee, Father and Son and Spirit, praise and glory and honor, world without end, Amen.

GREETING

FROM THE MOTHER CHURCH

BY REV. T. F. [...] OF IPSWICH

PREFATORY REMARKS.

Beloved Children, Fathers and Mothers:

If I speak to you with somewhat of deliberateness you will bear me witness that, after the story of this morning, it becomes any representative of the First Parish Church of Ipswich to be a little careful in his utterance. I have my notes in my hand as you see, but I find myself in sympathy with a public speaker of whom I once heard who "wanted to make a few remarks, before he began to speak."

In answer to the question jocosely put to your pastor as to what he wanted me to say on this occasion, I received the kindly suggestion, that I might say "anything I pleased, if only it was appropriate." To speak is less difficult sometimes than to speak appropriately. Pope long ago said: "Fools rush in where angels fear to tread." And though the fourteenth in that succession of preachers and pastors whose brilliant beginning was so clearly brought to our view by the first speaker of the day, it may be that I am to show myself one of the "fools;" first, for consenting to address, ever so briefly, an audience already filled and delighted with the interesting and admirable historical and biographical addresses of the morning; and secondly, for attempting to hold the attention of those who have been exposed to the temptations of such sumptuous tables as we have just left; and again, in the esteem of some, for presuming to say any thing in this presence in behalf of Ipswich. In my own estimate the latter reason is without force. It is true that I had hardly left the platform this morning before such salutations as these met me. "I wonder what you can say now for Ipswich." "I am glad I have not got your job on my hands." "I would not be in your shoes" "&c." But, friends, I am here on an errand of good-will from the mother church. I am not set for the defense of "Brother Hubbard" or any other man. I can share fully in the joy of this hour, for every honorable word that can justly be spoken of this ancient church, reflects its glory back upon the older mother. The Child can receive no genuine honor or blessing in which the parent does not share.

The "prodigal son" was an occasion of pain to his father as he went out to a life of recklessness and shame, but when he "came to himself" and began to live worthily and to promise better things, there was joy in the father's heart, and good cheer in the home, because the "son" was restored. So the honor of our offspring is ours as well, and we are not disposed to forego our claim.

Then further, you are having the Essex church anniversary to-day and the Chebacco phase of the history is prominent. Next year we hope to hold the two hundred and fiftieth anniversary of the organization of the Ipswich church, and the mother side of the story may appear.

If not many are here from the old Church, it is not because of any desire to avoid the record of an earlier day, for our earlier records are lost, said to have been burned. Whether in anything said here there is suggested to any a reason for their destruction, or not, I will not venture one, but invite you to the assigned duty of the moment.

ADDRESS.

As with dim-visioned Isaac of old in the hands of a scheming wife, so there is with me to-day a conflict of the senses. The witness of voice and hand is not one. Almost in the same breath I find myself sharing in the life of two strongly contrasted periods.

The force of the morning thought has been such as to take us back into the seventeenth century, but the order which has bidden us go from this spot and look upon fair fields and goodly dwellings on our way to the populous village of the dead, and has spread before us in such profusion the viands and the cheer of what was modestly named in the programme a "collation," and which summons us now to words of congratulation rather than of reminiscence, recalls us to our advanced standing in the nineteenth century. And I am bound to recognize the higher authority of the modern fact. The mandate of your committee of arrangements permits me neither to philosophize nor dream.

I am asked to present greetings from the Mother Church; and yet, cheerfully as I renew the pledges of interest in, and high desire for, the peace, and purity, and prosperity of this "revolted province" of our once wide First Parish "dominion" —pledges given many times between the old style Aug. 12, 1685, and the present hour, in cordial response to the summons for counsel or sympathy or mutual labor and joy in the Lord—the truth is, and I may as well out with it at the start, that I find the maternal sense in myself exceedingly small. Even though a representative of the church in whose fellowship your fathers and ours knew the ministry of Ward and Morton and Rogers and Cobbett and Hubbard, I must humbly confess that my representative capacity does not intensify my maternal sensibility.

As a pastor of eight years standing only—though in that time I have known personally one numerical third of your stated ministry for the whole two centuries of your church life — you will not wonder that any excess of sentiment in me must be forced, when you remember what changes time has wrought in outward conditions as well as in men.

You will not fail to see this first, that the names our church records cherish in common are comparatively few. Of these it is a little remarkable that the name of one of your foremost men, Mr. Cogswell, should have been associated with the last diaconate in the mother church, made vacant by death, a name dear in the educational and religious life of Ipswich and still with the old prefix, "John," at the official head of our Sunday School. But this is one of the few exceptions.

In the second place, if there is frequent social intercourse between the First and Second Parishes, I do not know it. The old system of "Quarterly Fasts," which would not let the brethren and sisters of one stock forget their kinship if they were so inclined, are long ago things of the past. It was months after his coming here before I learned of the presence of the acting pastor of to-day, and it is only three days since I had first sight of his person. The more shame to me is it? Well, consider the third fact namely this, that the multiplication of churches about us in these years has called for such a change in the limits of our local conferences, that there are no annual opportunities for meeting one another. The same thing is true of our ministerial association.

Then, further, the two parishes have *no business interests* in common. Ipswich as a shire town is no more, so that there is little to draw Chebacco to Agawam; and what attracts Agawam to Chebacco, unless it be a Bi-centennial Anniversary, or a Bi-ennial Ecclesiastical Council, attracts *through* it, to busy Gloucester or Manchester-by-the-Sea.

So far then as any blood concern goes, this work of mine is a pleasant fiction. In their practical relation to the kingdom of Christ on earth, the churches of Haverhill and Ipswich know more of each other than do we.

We are met here to-day because two hundred years ago, honest men God-fearing men, could not altogether agree; because, (and I quote the words of a man of precious memory among you, the father of the historian of the morning,) because "the children less sensible of the value of religious privileges than their fathers and mothers who thought but little of the tediousness of the way to the house of God, were less inclined to make so great a sacrifice to enjoy them."

The sincere congratulations of this hour are not the narrow ones of a household, but the broad ones of the great brotherhood in Christ, tinctured, colored, flavored, not with the recollection, but with the historical assurance, of this, that so many years ago our predecessors worshiped under one roof, paid a parish tax into the same treasury, brought their children to the same font for baptism, and around a common table received the consecrated elements from the same hands.

If now we could transfer ourselves to that early day and speak to those "children" impatient not of their old fellowship, but of the "tediousness of the way," we might banter them a little upon their faint-heartedness. We might report to them the great disturbance and the consuming grief of the mother church that having in the persons of their fathers walked with us in the ways of the Lord, for fifty years, they could not have continued to do so the little matter of two hundred years or so longer.

We might deplore the effect upon themselves of substituting for the heroic buffeting of wind and storm, and the treading of the uphills and the downhills, between this spot and the Center, the tame measuring of a few paces on foot or in carriage to a meeting house so "handy by"—and we might add to the sum of our reproach, the force of their example, by which those (with *us* or *you*) who learned of their reluctance to go six *miles* to the Sanctuary, have strengthened themselves in the refusal to go as many rods, unless the conditions are *as* favorable, at least, for seeing and being seen, as for God's worship.

And yet, however sorely we might have to reproach this faction for the folly of sundering the maternal leading strings, and setting up in life on their own account, we should have to confess, by all the tokens this morning afforded, that the first step taken after the separation, in the choice of a pastor, was an eminently wise one, followed, as the record shows, by many another. And all these not exhaustive of the stock of wisdom native to this region, as the self-conceit of the moment allows me to find suggested in the name of the present minister here, and as I hope the event may abundantly and happily prove.

But, beloved, we have no such word of reproof as a deliberate departure from the companionship of the trying beginnings of religious life here might, under some conditions, justify. We have no greater desire or joy, than that you "our children walk in the truth."

If, in the later past, the feet of our membership have not been turned in this direction, except on special occasions, remember that when the daughter makes for herself a home away from the parental roof, it is her province to seek the old home, it is hers to trust that there is always mother love there and to draw upon it, while the mother guiding the old house, limits her visits to seasons of a character unusual because of the great joy or sorrow in them. So we have visited you in your affliction, and extended our felicitations in your joy. If, when your councils were divided, we could not suit you all, you must consider the weakness for a grandchild which not even churches, as it appears, escape; and you must also bear witness that your afterwards united counsels awakened gladness in the heart of my honored predecessor, "Parson Kimball," and his beloved people. They were here with their prayers and benedictions, when the spirit of God persuaded your fathers "how good and how pleasant a thing it is for brethren to dwell together in unity." It was said concerning the parish division here, "conclusive proof was afforded that there had been little, if any, personal alienation of feeling between the individual members of the two bodies." The same might with truth have been said of the earlier separation in whose anniversary we now share.

In the pursuit of my pastoral work from the edge of Hamilton on one side to the borders of Rowley on the other, I have not happened to fall in with any of the participants in those warm discussions which issued in sending delegations to the general Court. Nor, as Artemas Ward said of George Washington, do I know that I have found anybody "wearing their old clothes."

Certainly I have found no person commissioned to speak for them in reference to the occurrences of this day. But I have become familiar with the foundation work they did. I have heard somewhat of the "manner of Spirit they were of." I have seen enough to assure me that if they were to-day in the flesh, they would, with us, rejoice in all your joy, as it is pleasant to think that, in another sphere, they give each other cordial greeting as they look back upon the follies, and the forbearances of day before yesterday afternoon.

In cordial fellowship with them, we, their successors in the occupancy and conduct of the old estate, discerning clearly that there is work enough for us all to do without laying the constraint of so much as a protest upon each other, give you to-day and henceforth our "God-speed."

We congratulate you upon the large common sense resident in the men and women of 1683, even with its admixture of a shrewdness, which enabled them to get their first meetinghouse raised without subjecting themselves to the penalty of a disregarded injunction from the "great and general Court."

We congratulate you upon all the work God has, through your fathers and their children, wrought here.

We congratulate you upon your ministry to the broader world without, wrought through those who were cradled in your Essex church homes, consecrated at your altars, educated in your schools, spiritually trained under your godly ministry, the lawyers, the doctors, the teachers, the ministers of the Lord Jesus Christ, a goodly company, part on earth, part in glory.

We congratulate you upon your present numerical strength, upon your acceptable ministry, upon your opportunities for Christian work, and the promise you hold in common with us all of the Master's living and helpful presence, and we pray that you may worthily hold the prestige God's providence has given you, and transmit it unimpaired to the generation which a hundred years hence shall gather as we now do in grateful recognition of the redeeming and sanctifying grace of Jesus Christ, their Lord and ours.

Greeting

FROM THE SISTER CHURCHES

It seems like trespassing, Mr. President, for me to take any of the precious time that belongs to this pleasant family gathering. But I have noticed that when a florist gathers a boquet he goes outside of his green house for ferns or grasses for its background, and so sets off the beauty of his choice flowers by way of contrast. With the thought that your committee wanted something *green* or *dry* from the outside world to serve as a background for the better display of the rare and beautiful products of this goodly garden of Essex, I have been persuaded to say a few words.

It is not too much to say that I was delighted with the exercises of the morning. Such addresses are wonderfully stimulating and instructive, not only to those personally interested, but to all that are students of history. I have long known that this church was founded by a *Wise* master builder, but how wise and illustrious he was I had no conception until his services and exploits were set before us by the Dexterous pen of our Nestor of Congregationalism.

As soon as I came into this neighborhood I discovered that this church was regarded by the others of the conference with wonder and admiration because of the number of educated men and women it has sent out from its borders, but after listening to the remarkably clear and discriminating historical address this morning, I am compelled to believe that this elder sister has not been half appreciated. I had supposed that when "the flower of Essex," was massacred at Bloody Brook, that the whole county met with an irretrievable loss, but I think I have discovered to-day that the root of that "flower" was planted in this church and that its vigorous growth since that time has not only made that great loss good, but has provided many distinguished men for the whole Commonwealth.

With such a history so rich and varied, so suggestive and helpful it is eminently appropriate that you should celebrate your two hundredth anniversary. I will not occupy the time with my personal congratulations though they are most abundant and sincere. I will not detain you with the greetings which my church extend to you to-day. The number who have come over to these exercises indicates our interest in this occasion and we are free to confess that we owe to you as a church a debt of gratitude that we can never repay. But I come before you as a representative of the churches of this conference and bring their warmest greetings to this elder sister elect, precious. We are glad of this privilege of expressing our congratulations for such an honorable record. It falls to the lot of many good men and women never to know how highly they are appreciated by their associates. The words of commendation due, are not spoken until their bodies are robed for the grave. But such a church anniversary as this, gives an opportunity for expressions of interest and respect on the part of those who have long recognized the worth of a beloved sister in the Lord.

Your history as a church is a noble one and though you can not boast of a written record of a thousand years, yet it requires no spirit of prophecy to say *such* a record is before you.

It is especially fitting at this time to extend to this elder sister the right hand of fellowship which has been given so many times by you to the younger members of this family of churches as they sprung into existence. We esteem it a great favor that we can to-day express our gratitude for your loving kindness and faithful efforts in our behalf. The fellowship of the churches is the crowning glory of our denomination. It is not a mere sentiment about which words abundant and meaningless may be spoken; it is not a vague theory beautiful in outline but of no value in practical experience; it is not simply coming together in council when we meet to install or dismiss a pastor; it is not restricted to the pleasant relation which exists in the association of churches in conference or that opens the way for the exchange of neighboring pastors, but it is the spirit of mutual sympathy and cooperation that permeates our relation to each other and holds us with a power like that which keeps the planets in their course about the sun. While we are independent of each other in the matter of our creed and are free to act our own pleasure concerning the work of the individual church, yet this invisible bond of common interests and affection gives a feeling of responsibility for the material and spiritual welfare of the whole sisterhood of churches, which is of most vital importance to our growth and prosperity.

The word sister, has a most significant meaning as applied to our relation to each other as churches. It suggests the charming picture which greets the eye in many well regulated homes, where the elder sister takes a motherly interest in the younger members of the household, and anticipates their wishes and happiness at the cost of great self denial. Such has been the interest which the older churches have taken in their younger sisters. Churches that were formed fifty years ago and more, came into existence under peculiarly distressing circumstances. When the Evangelical Church at Gloucester was born, the Mother Church looked upon its offspring as one born out of due time and possessed neither ability or willingness to nurse it as its own. This weak and helpless infant, an orphan from birth, would have been left to the tender mercies of a cold unfeeling world had not the sisterly impulses of the churches at Essex and Sandy Bay led them to take the child and nourish it for the Lord.

Had it not been for Dr. Crowell and Rev. David Jewett aided by the churches they represented, that little church at Gloucester Harbor could never have survived the trials of its earliest years. These two men were not only interested in the formation of the church but in securing for it the stated means of grace. They arranged to have the pulpit supplied by neighboring ministers until they could obtain a pastor to take up the work. They both labored faithfully to secure a shelter for the homeless orphan and were on the building committee which erected the first church edifice. The building cost two thousand dollars of which only four hundred were contributed by the little band of believers, for the balance of the debt these two men became personally responsible until they secured it by repeated solicitation from the stronger churches of the state.

The interest of these neighboring pastors extended to the spiritual growth and prosperity of the church. As soon as a minister was installed they united with him in holding a protracted meeting which brought a large addition to the church. When difficulties and dissensions arose they were ready with their wise and faithful counsel to promote harmony and unity of feeling. One instance is on record where they were called to advise concerning some difficulty with the pastor and the whole church voted by rising, "that the difficulties be here dropped, and that the person hereafter making them matter of conversation shall be considered as violating the peace of the church."

But Dr. Crowell and his associates were not only interested in the church at Gloucester Harbor, but they did a similar work at Lanesville, at West Gloucester, at North Beverly, at Saugus and I know not how many other places. It is simply amazing to find how much these men did outside of their own special field of labor. They were large hearted, far seeing men, the circle of their endeavor was not bounded by the narrow horizon of their own parish, they took into their sympathetic hearts the spiritual wants of every needy village in the community about them. They were illustrious examples of the Christian activity to which reference was made in the historical address.

It is one of the great advantages of such a celebration as this, that a church finds out as in no other way what has been done in the past worthy of imitation. It is quickened by the review of such devotion and moved to thank God and take courage. This church will be all the stronger for the next one hundred years for the story that has been told to-day. The spirit that animated the ministry fifty years ago, is needed in these times; we should cultivate a wider vision and a deeper love for the cause of Christ. We ought to see the waste places about us that may be made with God's blessing to bud and blossom as the rose. We ought to be willing as churches to deny ourselves of our rights and privileges that the Gospel may be preached to the benighted beyond our borders. As our minds thrill to-day with the story of the results of the lives of those who have made the history of this church and town, let us all profit by these lessons and return to our work with a renewed purpose to do more and better work for Christ.

Reminiscences of Dr. Crowell

BY REV. JEREMIAH TAYLOR, D. D., OF PLYMOUTH, L. I.

Mr. Chairman, Fathers and Brethren:

It seems appropriate that I should be with you on this interesting occasion, for several reasons. A descendant of one of the honored pastors of this church sustained to me the relation of a beloved sister as the wife of my brother; and the pastor of your neighboring church at Manchester; Rev. Oliver Alden Taylor. How often have I listened to the glowing descriptions she gave of her grandfather and the eminent service he rendered the church and state while pastor here. And it would be a profitable service, did time permit to trace the influence of the honored men who have served you here so long and so well, not merely in the confines of this parish, but on the broader range of the Community at large. Rev. John Cleaveland, gave to this County an eminent physician in the person of his son, Nehemiah Cleaveland, M. D., whose public life was identified, with the varied interests which entered into the growth of Topsfield. Of his four sons, brothers of my sister, one was a bright ornament of the legal profession; and spent his life in connection with the Bar of New York. Another was a distinguished clergyman, and boldly and successfully defended the doctrines of our faith, in the face of great opposition in one of the New England cities and left a work nobly done for the church. Another became an ornament in the department of literature, and the fourth was known and honored in the manufacturing and agricultural industry of this native county. Rare men all.

A good deal of interest also has been awakened on my part to see how my friend, the present pastor in charge of this venerable pulpit wreathed with the crown of two centuries, may carry himself. It was my pleasure to greet him when he took his ordination vows, and we would gladly have retained him in the field where he was then installed.

But the chief thing which has brought me here is to say a few things in regard to one of the later pastors of the church who is so well remembered by the older portion of the congregation, Rev. Robert Crowell, D.D.

When called in 1847 to take the pastorate of the neighboring church at Wenham; I took advise of your pastor as to the course of duty, and he as much as any one influenced the final decision.

And when for the ordination services the Ecclesiastical Council was called, and parts were finally assigned, on him devolved the duty of giving the charge to the young pastor. It impressed me then as a most excellent address of its kind, and as the parts were published, I have had opportunity to read it often since, and now think it to be a model both in regard to instruction and style. During the years, in which neighborly, pastoral relations existed between us, I had occasion to meet him often under circumstances, that could not fail to reveal the spirit of the man.

Attempting to walk over to Manchester of a Sabbath morning to fulfil an appointment for an exchange, he slipped on the ice and brook his leg. Paying him a visit as he lay upon his couch in consequence of this disabled condition; in perfect calmness, and a spirit of gentle resignation he said I have often questioned whether I was in the place of duty, but I have now no doubt, as I lie here, that I am just where God has put me.

When in December 1851, my brother of Manchester died, there was no question as to whom he would wish to have preach his funeral discourse, I hastened in my grief to Dr. Crowell and engaged him for that service. The day of burial however proved so severe in cold and storm that he deemed it unsafe to leave his home, but delivered the sermon to the bereaved people on a subsequent Sabbath to the satisfaction of all concerned. Of Dr. Crowell personally I was impressed that he was loyal to *himself*. He cultivated those habits of life and character which brought him into close fellowship with God. The saint appeared clearly in the man. No one could be in his company for however short a time without feeling that he was spiritually minded; holy beyond what is ordinary. He was loyal to the *letter* of the Sacred Scriptures. He was a thorough student of the Word. Not content with his private studies of the original tongues, he in company with several others of the pastors in the vicinity formed what they called a Sub-Association, and met frequently to read and discuss together the Greek and Hebrew text.

He was also loyal to the *doctrines* of that Word; what the Scriptures taught satisfied. He was not led, by any speculations a step beyond, and when it is remembered who were his associates in the neighboring pastorates during his later years, one is not easily persuaded to believe there were essential doctrines in the Sacred Word which they had not discovered and the need of any departure from the faith which was then taught does not commend itself as worthy of serious regard. Those were the days, when Gale was at Rockport, Taylor at Manchester, Abbott at Beverly, Braman at Danvers, Worcester and Emerson at Salem, Cooke at Lynn, and the pulpit gave no uncertain instruction under their ministrations. Oh! for the return of an era of such long and able pastorates when the preacher will have time and opportunity, as then, to teach his people thoroughly the profound things of life and salvation.

Dr. Crowell evinced a deep interest in young ministers, he had a happy way in conversation of calling out their opinions on abstruse and difficult topics, carefully concealing his own judgment to the last, when by a brief utterance he made abiding his own clear convictions in the mind of the listener. I have brought to this hour the results of a conversation I once held with him on the views of the elder President Edwards in regard to the social ostracism of excommunicated church members. In counsel Dr. Crowell was regarded excellent, highly acceptable as a preacher, ever welcome to the pulpits of neighboring parishes.

It was in 1855, that we assembled in the house of God where he had so long preached the gospel, to honor him in burial. Thence we bore his mortal remains to the neighboring cemetery, committing them earth to earth, ashes to ashes, dust to dust, there to rest with his sleeping congregation and arise with them in triumphant, glorious resurrection.

Brethren, we seem standing to-day in exalted contemplation with the apostle when he exclaims in the opening verses of the twelfth chapter of Hebrews: "Wherefore seeing we also are compassed about with so great a cloud of witnesses, let us lay aside every weight and the sin which doth so easily beset us, and let us run with patience the race that is set before us, looking unto Jesus the author and finisher of our faith." And especially let us take heart in view of the concluding portion of the chapter: "Wherefore, we receiving a kingdom which cannot be moved, let us have grace whereby we may serve God acceptably with reverence and godly fear. For our God is a consuming fire."

LETTERS.

PARIS, July 14, 1883.

My Dear Brother,— I promised to write you a brief line expressing my interest in the two hundredth anniversary of the founding of the Essex Church, occuring Aug. 22. I was unable to write before leaving Boston, and since landing at Liverpool have had no good opportunity until the present. Our stay has been brief, in places visited, until we reached London, and we have had much to see and think about. We have really been living, quite as much in England and Scotland of *the past*, as of the present. We visited Ambleside and Grasmere; the *home*, the church and grave of Wordsworth; Glasgow and Stirling; saw places sacred to the memory of Bruce and Wallace and Douglass; the fields of Stirling and Bannockburn; Melrose and Dryburg Abbeys, and Abbottsford, the home with the Library of Sir Walter Scott, as he left it; Edinburgh with its Castle and its Holy Rood and Memories of Mary Queen of Scotts, the rooms where she lived in part her singularly tragic life; the house, pulpit and chair of John Knox, the grand old scottish reformer; the old town of York with its Minster, its relics of Roman days and honored as the birth-place of Constantine; then London with so much to see, and now *Paris*. In the brief time alloted, I am striving to review the past as well as study the present. Do you wonder I have not much time save as I snatch a few minutes here and there to write.

To-day all Paris is alive. It is the Anniversary of the taking of the Bastile. I have been this morning to a grand review of Troops (in Bois de Boulogne).

Poor France is struggling to maintain a Republic, but on the one hand the struggle is between the repressed elements of parties that have had well nigh centuries of history and bloodshed, and on the other, not between Catholicism and Protestanism, I wish it were, *then* there would be more hope of grand fulfilment, but between Catholicism and Atheism. The Government is largely Atheistic. President Grevy is a noble looking man, we saw him to-day drive by us on his way to the Boulogne. But I am told he is Atheistical, indeed religious instruction is taken from the schools, and the name of God even *may* be expunged from the school books, and yet boys of ten years are required to learn the use of the *sword* and *bayonet*. Paris is a beautiful city. Some have named it "The American Paradise." The contrast with England is marked. The almost absolute cleanliness of streets, and Boulevards, the tinting and coloring every where, the excitability of speech and movement, show a different people. There is an absence of English stability. To-day is the unveiling of the Statue of Liberty, so long in preparation, and it is done with a clash between the Government of Paris and that of the Republic. Soldiers are posted to keep back the mob, and the President of the Republic withholds his presence.

But I turn for a little while as a privilege from all this, to the scenes, faces and memories of dear old Essex. The Town I remember best is that of twenty years ago. It is no wonder I love to hold in memory those who had so much to do, outside the home, in moulding my own life. Pardon me if I speak of a few personal things. Deep in my heart do I keep the memory of my two boyhood pastors— the first, while striving personally to interest me and aid me in a course of study, which after the lapse of years I was enabled to pursue, did not fail to set before me, the claims of God on my life. The second led me to Christ, was to me brother and pastor and opened the way, for my then maturer years, to enter the Christian Ministry. I remember with gratitude that Superintendent ; that man who did so much for Christ's kingdom in the Sabbath School, that man, who knew how to educate, and not only laid the foundation of christian character in his pupils but made theologians of them. I remember the three Sabbath School teachers, the last of whom led his class like a good shepherd. They are all gone to the Spirit land,—and so to have that wider circle, many of whom were closely and dearly related, and some of them recently called. Many a face, many a voice comes to me to-night in this great city of another continent, and my memories are tender. But you in review will go back to earliest days, before the town had its present name, and to such men as Wise and others, who helped to make the first pages of religious history in "Chebacco." Two hundred years ! Why you are within eighty years of Brewster and his Scrooby church, "the model," Professor Hoppin tells us, "of all our New England churches to-day !" A few days ago, I passed on the rail, within a short distance of this "Spiritual birth place of America" and I confess I would rather have visited this "modern Nazareth" than St. Paul's or even Westminister in London. Scrooby and Brewster's church is not so very far behind your early history.

John Robinson and the Speedwell and May Flower are a little nearer. But go back a step in history. Side by side in the Museum of Edinburgh are the pulpit of John Knox, and the Guillotine, on which the old Scottish Covenanters were beheaded, I thanked God as I looked upon them for the brave men that battled the storm. But Knox and Calvin and kindred spirits clasped hands, and in the battle for the truth such spirits make a history. Come down now, from those days, a century later, and men like Brewster, and John

Robinson *will* rise, and driven out of England by persecution, with the pressure of centuries and Providence behind them, they *will* under God's lead find a Plymouth Rock,—Congregationalism!! No other *ism* was to be tolerated in a new world by the Pilgrims. All else was left behind—A scion of that *mighty root* was borne to your dear old town and planted in faith and carefully and prayerfully nourished. It took root and has grown. The fruitage we can see. Plymouth Rock has done for Essex mentally, morally and spiritually, what eternity alone will reveal. I revere the names you will revere to-day. I am greatly disappointed not to be with you to assure you in person of my own interest in the church and to listen to those who will address you. They will dwell upon much that binds us together in the work, for Christ, past and present. What a difference in the progress of the Gospel *among all nations* since John Wise, was called home— (I congratulate you my brother on your happy relation with that dear people) God bless the dear old Church. I am with you in spirit though far away. Accept my heartiest wishes and sincere prayers for the success of your plans to-day.

Read of this what you desire and believe me,

Your brother in Christ,
MICHAEL BURNHAM.

ROWLEY, Aug. 2, 1883.

My Dear Sir,—The letter from yourself and your associates inviting me to be present at your celebration, came during my absence from home, and it must not be left longer unnoticed.

My associations with your church are exceedingly pleasant, where I used to preach that Gospel upon which as a corner stone, the fathers and the children have rested their hopes. Many lively and choice stones have gone into that building which was begun among you two hundred years ago, and which will not reach its completion, and show its utmost beauty till the Lord shall come.

Your Pastor Rev. Mr. Crowell, I had but little intercourse with, except in an occasional exchange, but know him to have been a man of God, who had a system of faith which was not the less desirable to him because it had been the faith of the centuries, and with no sentiment of which he thought it needful to part in order to make the rest more defensible, and the light of which was like that of the sun, brightest and best when all its colors were preserved and blended.

With the shorter pastorate of Rev. Mr. Bacon, I was somewhat acquainted, and regarded him as a man who preached faithfully the gospel he professed to love, and devoted himself to the interests of the people who were committed to his care.

There was one I used to meet, David Choate, whom to know once is always to remember, whose life was an "epistle known and read of all men," and who will have as large a proportion as we can well conceive any one to have, of children whom he has instructed and guided, and over whom he will be permitted to say to the Master at the last, here am I, and the children thou hast given me.

These, and other considerations, rather incline me to answer affirmatively your invitation. I have, however, a life infirmity which I did not have when I used to mingle with those who are gone and who still remain among you, which anchors me quite strongly to my home when public occasions would call me away. It has been somewhat increased by my return last month to the College where I graduated fifty years ago, and where I felt obliged to take certain responsibilities for my Class which my strength hardly warranted, and which make it uncertain whether it is suitable for me, so soon, to go again into a public assembly where my mind and heart would be much excited and interested. I propose, therefore, not to positively decline, but to let the matter be under consideration until I shall see whether the increasing inflammation of my eyes is likely to be more troublesome and permanent. If I am able to come shall probably bring with me the two members of my family who, having shared the griefs of my home, I shall desire to share with me in all the interest your glad occasion may impart.

Very truly yours,
J. PIKE.

To Caleb S. Gage and others, Committee
of First Church and Parish, Essex.

The following sketch of Mr. Webster was read by Mr. Palmer before the reading of the letter from Rev. J. C. Webster. See Hist. Essex p. 263.

"Nov. 13, 1799 Rev. Josiah Webster was ordained pastor of the church as successor to Mr. Cleaveland. Rev. Stephen Peabody, of Atkinson N. H. preached the ordination sermon.

In 1806, having requested a dismission, a mutual council is called, and by their advice his pastoral relation is dissolved on the 23 of July.

The reason for this action was briefly as follows. At Mr. Webster's settlement the parish gave him $500 as a donation, or settlement as it was called. His annual salary was $334 and the parsonage. As the currency diminished in value his salary became insufficient. The parish voted to allow $100 from year to year as should be found necessary. The pastor was satisfied with the amount of this addition but insisted that it should be made a part of the orignal contract. The parish thought their pastor should have confidence in their good will to vote the addition yearly along with the rest of the salary. It was upon this issue that the pastoral relation was dissolved at Mr. Webster's request.

He was afterwards settled in Hampton, N. H. June 8, 1808 where after a quiet and successful ministry he died March 27, 1837, aged 65.

In the twelfth vol. of the American Quarterly Register there is a biographical sketch of him from which these extracts have been taken.

"Rev. Josiah Webster, the son of Nathan and Elizabeth Webster was born in Chester, N. H. Jan. 16, 1772.

His father was a farmer, barely in circumstances of comfort, with patient, laborious industry, providing for the wants of a large family, and therefore unable to furnish more than a common school education for his children.

Josiah, the eldest, in his 16th year went to reside with an uncle, whose affairs he managed in his many and long absences. But for a long time he had felt a strong desire to become a minister of the gospel, and though he had acquired only sufficient property to defray the expenses of preparation for college, and was distressed and discouraged by the opposition of his friends, in his 19th year he repaired to the Rev. Mr. Remington, of Candia, under whose hospitable roof he began his studies. Afterwards he spent a year under the tuition of that eminent Christian, Rev. Dr. Thayer of Kingston, and completed his preparation at the Academy in Atkinson. It was at Kingston that he indulged the hope of reconciliation to God, and of the commencement of the Christian life. A deeper consciousness of sin than he had ever felt before, pressed upon his heart, so full of distress and alarm that for several days he was unable to pursue his studies. After a season of deep conviction, light broke out upon his mind, like a morning of Summer just as the sun rises, when the winds are hushed, and a solemn but delightful stillness prevails everywhere and the face of nature smiles with verdure and flowers.

From Atkinson he took a journey of more than eighty miles to Dartmouth College, for the mere purpose of examination and admission to college. His poverty prevented his remaining a single week to enjoy its advantages. Returning to Atkinson he pursued his studies under the instruction of the preceptor Stephen P. Webster, until the Spring of 1795, when with little improvement in the state of his funds he rejoined his class in College, and completed his first year. At the close of the vacation, though disappointed in every effort to raise money among his friends he once more set his face toward College. By a mysterious providence of God he fell in company with a stranger, who, learning his condition, without solicitation offered to relieve his necessities by a loan of money to be repaid whenever his circumstances should permit. The traveler was afterward ascertained to be a merchant of Newburyport. After graduating in the year 1798, he studied theology with Rev. Stephen Peabody, the minister of Atkinson, about a year, and was then licensed to preach the gospel by the Haverhill Association. Soon after he was invited to preach as a candidate in Chebacco Parish, Ipswich, where, Nov. 1799, he was ordained. After his dismission from that pastorate on account of the inadequacy of his support, he was invited to preach to the church at Hampton, N. H., and was installed there, June 8, 1808. During his ministry at Hampton there were several revivals of religion, as the fruit of which one hundred and seventy persons were gathered into the church.

It deserves to be recorded to the lasting honor of Mr. Webster that he perceived the evil effects of the use of ardent spirits at a period when even the eyes of good men were generally closed to the subject. Almost from the first of his ministry he preached against intemperance, and for years before the temperance reformation, observed entire abstinence from all that intoxicates.

He was also deeply interested in the cause of education. To his influence and agency, the Academy in Hampton, one of the most respectable and flourishing institutions in the State, is indebted for much of its character and usefulness.

Attached to the faith and institutions of our fathers, the doctrines of grace he understood and loved, and preached to the very close of his life. His last public act was the preaching of the sermon at the ordination of his son Rev. John C. Webster at Newburyport, as seaman's preacher at Cronstadt Russia March 15, 1837. Anxious to perform the service assigned him on that occasion, he made an effort his impared health was unable to sustain. The day following he returned home, and taking his bed remarked that he thought his work on earth was done. 'Well' said he 'if it be so, I know not with what act I could close life with more satisfaction.' He died of inflammation of the lungs. During his sickness, his mind was often alienated, but in lucid intervals he uniformly expressed confidence in the mercy of God, and cast himself upon the blood of atonement.

His funeral sermon, preached by the Rev. Dr. Dana, is highly commendatory of his ministerial qualifications, devotion to his proper work, and his extensive usefulness. Mr. Webster published five discourses delivered on different occasions."

WHEATON, ILL., Aug. 3, 1883.

REV. F. H. PALMER: *Dear Brother*,—Though I am a personal stranger to you, and probably, to all in your church and parish, allow me to express my interest in the two hundredth anniversary of your church, which I notice is at hand, from the fact that my father was pastor of it the first six years of the present century. And though he left Essex, then Chebacco parish in Ipswich, before I was born, some of my earliest and very pleasant reminiscences are with your town. The names of its Choates, Lows, Burnhams and others were household words in our family during all the first years of my life. And I know my father carried to his grave the fondest remembrance of many of the associations of that, his first pastoral love.

I may, therefore, be excused for thinking it not inappropriate to contribute, for use as it may be thought best, a few extracts from letters in my possession, written years ago, indicative of the kind and high esteem in which my father was held by some of his parishioners, who were natives or citizens of Essex, whose professional and national reputation has scarcely been excelled, and of whom the town may very justly be proud.

Under date, Cincinnati Ohio, Dec. 5, 1856, R. D. Mussey M. D. one of the most distinguished physicians and surgeons of the U. S. wrote as follows:

"My first acquaintance with him was in the parish of Ipswich, now Essex, Mass., while he was the pastor of the church in that place. It was in great measure due to his efficient friendship that, young and inexperienced, I gained an early introduction to professional practice. No spirit of jealousy, envy or concealment seemed to have found a place in the bosom of Mr. Webster. * * And now after the lapse of fifty years, the impressions of his cordial salutations, whether at his home or on the street, made with a firm grasp of the hand, a rich and benignant smile often accompanied with the announcement of some item of intelligence on a topic of mutual interest, comes up with the freshness of yesterday.

As a preacher, Mr. Webster was solemn and impressive. His exhibitions of truth were clear, intelligible and direct, not encumbered with verboseness nor metaphysical subtilties, but adapted to the comprehension of all classes of hearers, and uttered with an earnestness and ardor, which showed how deeply he was impressed with the magnitude and responsibility of the gospel ministry."

Hon. David Choate, under date, Essex, April 18, 1870 wrote :

"The impressive yet affectionate solemnity of your father more especially *in*, but often *out* of the pulpit was a striking feature—how he would *glow* as he advanced both in prayer and preaching, rising from half inarticulate utterance to the full swellings of a rich and mellow voice, increasing frequently to the end. And then it was more especially that the grandure of the *Amen* was so overwhelming, *always* in the prayers, and, I think, always at the close of the sermon. And the *Amen*, I have never yet forgotten, was uttered, as a part of the prayer, and never as a *word added to it;* thus giving more than mortal significance to it * * * I have often times wished your father's manner in pronouncing the Amen might be revived. I have seen an audience so lifted up by it, so *filled* with it, that after its utterance he would himself be calmly occupying his seat long before the people began to sit down or could think he was done,—"they thought him still speaking, still stood firm to hear." I assure you this is no fancy sketch, it began in my childhood, I could never forget it: I never shall."

Hon. Rufus Choate wrote as follows from Boston, July 27, 1857:

"He had times of hearing the children of the parish in their catechism, and his appearance then and in the pulpit are all blended in my recollections, into one general impression of a certain dignity of goodness. What led to his dismissal I do not know * * * Three or four years afterward, passing that way he was invited to preach in his own pulpit, and the house was crowded as at an ordination, [which in those days, *meant* a crowd].

When boarding in his family for five or six months in 1815, [at Hampton, N.H.] while preparing for college, his kindness during all that time was so uniform, his councils regarding studies, deportment and a good life, so anxious, parental and wise, that I remember him as a son remembers his father, and would as little attempt an analysis of his character or critical estimate of his intellectual and professional claims and rank. * * In his general manner he was serious. He held the very highest tone of the orthodox opinions of his school and preached them without shade or accommodation. But his disposition was gentle and affectionate, his enjoyment of beauty in nature, music, literature and eloquence enthusiastic and tasteful; his occasional laugh unforced and most pleasant, and his conversation instructive and full of illustrative anecdote. I do not know what were the judgments of his clerical brethren, but, if I may trust my own distinct recollection, he was among the most graceful and most chaste of the elocutionists of the pulpit of that time and that Association."

Were it practicable, it would afford me great pleasure to be present at your celebration. It must be one of unusual historic and general interest. And I shall esteem it a great favor to receive from you any published account of it.

Very fraternally yours,
J. C. WEBSTER.

BOXFORD, Aug. 20th, 1883.

Gentlemen,— Accept my thanks for your kind invitation to be present on the interesting occasion you are to observe on the 22nd inst., an invitation with which I should gladly comply, if my health permitted.

Among the names, so far as my knowledge extends, which have rendered Essex memorable, two are very prominent— Crowell and Choate ("*par nobile fratrum*,") the one, for a long period pastor of the Church; the other, for several years, an officer in the Church and superintendent of the Sabbath School.

Dr. Crowell was in the prime of life when I, as a young man, first came to this town. From the very beginning of my acquaintance, I was led highly to esteem him. He was a sound and able preacher. I was accustomed to make a yearly exchange with him, and my people were always glad to see him in the pulpit.

Dea. Choate, besides possessing many other excellent qualities, I remember as peculiarly original and entertaining in his method of conducting the Sabbath School.

It may well be said of these sainted men that "Being dead, they yet speak." The blessed influence of their instructions and example will long be felt.

On the day you are to observe, mention will undoubtedly be made of many other worthies now in glory. May the occasion, and its results, be to you all that you can desire!

Yours very truly,

WM. S. COGGIN.

To Messrs. Gage, Cogswell, and others,
Committee of Church and Parish.

Sabbath School History.

In the absence of the Address on the Sabbath School which was expected at the Anniversary, the Church voted Oct. 23d, 1884 that the following Historical Address delivered at the Fiftieth Anniversary of the Sabbath School Dec. 26, 1881, by the Superintendent Dea. David Choate, be published in this volume.

Dear friends! twice five and twenty years ago!
Alas! how time escapes, — 'tis even so!

It was nearly in this manner, that the English Poet began his letter to his friend. He indeed had the lapse of only *once* that section of man's life to mourn,—we have it twice.

Whether on a review, our joy should be greater than his for having survived the longer campaign;—or whether our sorrow should overbalance for the reason that so many more have fallen by our side to renew the battles of life no more, it may not be easy to decide.

"Twice five and twenty years"! How difficult, how impossible to realize the flight of so vast a portion of human life! Do you ask, where is the age, the manhood, the maidens fair, the children sweet of fifty years ago? I should answer of all the *first*, and many of the second class, in the words of Doct. Daniel Hopkins heard here in my earliest boyhood, "They are all gone down into the grave, minister and all"! Do you ask after the *young men* and the *fair maidens*? Alas! the survivors of them have slid or are sliding into the arm-chair of life. And if the second generation of those "sweet *children*" are with us here to-day, what time of life I ask, do you think it is with *them*?

We are still however far, I apprehend, from appreciating all that is implied in the space of *fifty years*. Let us look a moment outside these venerated walls and see how the world itself has moved on since the first classes assembled around the newly ordained minister. Take a short walk about town. The same river still runs between the same banks. The same fine sheet of water, rolling down the same gentle Falls, still supplies it, thence rolling onward to the sea. You see the same woodlands and the same salt meadows — almost the same King-fisher and Robin seem to fly over us; — But with the exception of the unchanged face of unchanging nature, how changed is all beside! Old Chebacco becomes the namesake of the county. Her population more stationary than other things, has yet gone up from about twelve hundred to seventeen hundred, notwithstanding small but unreturning swarms have been going away from the parent hive. Two hundred dwelling houses, or nearly so, five school houses and two churches have been built and one remodeled. The little Pinkey of twelve to fifteen tons, drawn upon wheels, has become the tall schooner of 150 or 200. And as a fine comment upon the industry and economy of the people, the wealth of the town has advanced in these fifty years from $258,000 by the assessors' books in 1819, to $930,000 being three and six tenths times as great now as then.

A moments glance at the *outside* world may aid still further in taking in the great idea of fifty years. Since the day when one of the earliest Sabbath School Scholars whose step is still firm, repeated the 176 verses of the 119th Psalm, a thing never since done I believe at one lesson, every Railroad in America has been built.

The idea of a Telegraph wire either through the air or under the sea, had entered no man's mind until this Sabbath School had been in operation eighteen years. Within less than one half of the time of our Sabbath School existence Steam Power which had already one foot upon the land, has set the other down upon the sea. And although we may not say with Campbell, I believe, that "the Roman Empire has begun and ended" since that day, yet an empire larger by far than ever the Roman was, has been acquired by us and added to us. Since the early classes were assembled within these dear old walls, sixteen states have been added to the Union, while I deny that any have dropped out of it. Sixteen states I say of such magnitude as would make 164 like Massachusetts, besides territory enough to make six and thirty more. And while these lessons have been going on, we have seen thirteen Presidents of these United States. The country has endured twelve party conflicts, some of which have been nearly convulsive, and yet every one of them has subsided within a week after the struggle, as did the severest and the last.

Such is a glance at a few of the events that have transpired outside the Sabbath School room during the past fifty years. But I see and feel how inadequate all this has been to promote the object I have desired, and dismiss it with very little satisfaction.

The precise day and hour when our Sabbath School began to assemble around the old Pulpit cannot now be determined. The utter absence of Records is most painfully felt this day. The following statement of its origin however, collected from various conversations with the founder himself was read in his hearing July 4, 1849, and it is believed he approved it, as he made no objection to it either then or at any other time. The following is the language, "The experiment of organizing a Sabbath School in the town of Essex, then Chebacco, was first made by Rev. Robert Crowell, our present pastor, in the Summer of 1814, and within a few weeks after his ordination. He met the children, then thirty to forty in number, in the pews fronting the pulpit, at the ringing of the first bell in the morning, and heard them repeat verses of Scripture and Hymns. The school was discontinued through the Winter for several successive years."

It is known by documentary evidence, that the ordination referred to, took place on August 10, 1814, and the expression "within a few weeks after the ordination," would lead us to believe that in September or October the School began to assemble.

The earliest Record relating to the school known to exist is dated October 14, 1828, and reads as follows, viz.: "At a meeting of the Managers of the Essex Sabbath School, voted Samuel Burnham, Superintendent for one year: Voted that the following persons be requested to instruct in the Sabbath School for one year, viz.: J. S. Burnham, U. G. Spofford, Caleb Cogswell, Joseph Perkins, Zacheus Burnham, John Mears, Jr., William Henry Mears,—Louisa Crowell, Lucy Choate, Mary Boyd, Sally Burnham, Elizabeth Perkins, Lydia Perkins, Clara Perkins, Sally Bowers, Betsey Kinsman, Elizabeth Proctor: Voted David Choate Assistant Superintendent. And at a meeting of the Managers, Dec. 2, 1829, voted that there be two Superintendents, viz.: S. Burnham, and D. Choate."

It was also voted that there be two Librarians, viz.: U. G. Spofford and J. S. Burnham; the teachers of last year were re-chosen for one year more with the following in addition, Francis Burnham, Adoniram Story, Philemon S. Eveleth, Mrs. Hannah C. Crowell, Miss Abigail P. Choate, Mrs. Sally Burnham, Mrs. E. W. Choate, Mrs. Mina Burnham, Miss Sally Norton.

Twenty of the above twenty-seven teachers for these two years, were the fruits of the first revival of religion after the opening of the Sabbath School and which commenced late in the autumn of 1827.

No list of the members of the school for the first seventeen years can now be found. A full record however, of the members, in the hand writing of the Founder of the School, as it stood in 1831 has been carefully preserved, and is of much historical value. The whole number attending as pupils was then 140, of whom 84 had left when the present Superintendent began to act as such in the summer of 1837.

It would at first seem a natural division of a Historical sketch of the Sabbath School at the close of its 50th year, to take each of the five decades by itself. In the operations of the School however, there seems nothing particularly distinctive. One decade runs into another, and as there would be the unavoidable *overlapping*, and more especially as even the greatest latitude of time will require whole years to be crowded into a word, or omitted altogether, a running sketch of detached events is all that can be attempted, and not always regarding strictly chronological order, even then.

An uncertainty to us, hangs over the time when the change was made from simply committing Scripture, and a Question book was introduced. The first *written* evidence we have is the following. "At a Meeting of the Managers of the Sabbath School Oct. 14, 1828, it was voted to recommend 'Judson's Questions' for the use of the school and that brother Francis Burnham be a committee to procure two dozen of them." It seems probable that this was the first use of a Question Book, and they continued to be used until in July, 1843, their use was discontinued by vote of the teachers; and this discontinuance lasted through eleven consecutive years.

Our Sabbath School is the child of the Church. Although this idea has been sometimes repudiated, there is still evidence of its truth in our case the most abundant.

To say nothing of the fact, that the minister brought the school into existence, rocked it in its cradle, and carried it in his arms for whole years together, the Church itself as early as August, 1828, procured Watts' Catechism at its own expense, for the little ones of the school, and on the 7th of December, 1829, the Church voted to appropriate the sum of $15 for the purchase of a Library, and again on the 6th of May, 1832, eight dollars more for the same purpose. In Jan. 1838, the Church bought two dozen more Question Books, and three dozen Catechisms. The *great* expenditure for Bibles, begun in 1849, will be referred to again.

But if a cloud of uncertainty hangs over the time when committing Scripture exclusively gave way to the Question Book, a still deeper one rests upon the time when the transition of the School from the hands of its Founder, to those of its first Superintendent, Capt. Samuel Burnham, was made. Probably it was done gradually. That early Superintendent is not fully able to recollect the time when he first came into the School. *Female* teachers are believed to have heard the classes at first when the pastor was absent on exchange. The first male teachers were probably non-professors; indeed, they must have been; and with two or three exceptions this must have continued until the Revival of religion in 1828.

The learning and reciting of Watts' Psalms and Hymns in connection with the Bible lessons, was more popular with the School for the first five or six years, beginning in 1838, than it has been since. The 138th Hymn, 1st Book was quite a favorite, if we may judge from the number who committed it. The hymn commences with the verse—

"Firm as the earth, thy gospel stands,
My Lord, my hope, my trust;
If I am found in Jesus' hands,
My soul can ne'er be lost."

This Hymn was committed twenty-six years ago, and twenty-five out of the thirty-one who learned it, are believed to be still living. Of the six not living, some, we are certain, died in the undoubting belief that being "found in Jesus' hands their souls would ne'er be lost."

Among other hymns committed by the school during the years referred to, were those beginning

"Stand up my soul, shake off thy fears"—
"Life is the time to serve the Lord"—
"Thus far the Lord hath led me on"—
"There is a land of pure delight"—
"Lo! on a narrow neck of land"—
"Lord I am thine, but thou wilt prove
My faith, my patience, and my love."

These are only specimens, I give them by special request, as the recollection of them is dear to many hearts.

A call for volunteers in 1839 to read the Bible through without the offer of any reward whatever, was responded to by 136, not including teachers. These were all called on at two different times to report progress. A few (one certainly) had finished the whole before the first inquiry. How much was read after the *second* inquiry cannot now be known. Some, no doubt, left the great body of the book unread. But on summing up the chapters as given in by those who read, the number was 29,991 ;—equal to reading the whole Bible by 25 readers, with 272 verses to spare. All were charged to read names of persons and places with care. My belief is, that much of this reading was too rapid. Indeed, when in 1852, on the suggestion of a distinguished neighboring clergyman, a large number entered upon the plan of reading the Bible through in a year by reading three chapters on each and every week day, and five on every Sabbath, I became more than ever convinced that the reading was quite too *rapid* to derive lasting good from it. I have never encouraged such hasty reading since, and I probably never shall again.

If Dr. Taylor of Norwich could read the Epistle to the Romans through seventeen times, and never find the doctrine of Atonement in it, as he said he did, though it is admitted that his prejudice like an extinguisher upon a candle would be pretty effectual against receiving light from it, as Mr. Newton said was the case ;—yet I ask were not some of his readings probably too *rapid*, to admit of his discovering that pearl of great price?

I was about to speak of a system of class papers kept by the teachers for a few years, reporting the doings and conduct of the members, but must pass that with much other matter relating to the machinery of Sabbath Schools.

So of five pages of statistics, I must omit the details and give only a few results. Since our fourth of July celebration in 1859, when a full report was made, the school has contributed for benevolent purposes $442.99,—Expended at home on Libraries, library cases, and incidentals $185.

Reading for Soldiers $102. Missionary operations $109. Whole amount contributed, disbursed, mostly *abroad* since July 1849, back of which date I have not reckoned, $1015.72, leaving however a balance of $32.74 on hand.—I must omit all details of our numbers, except the fact that from and since 1831 when the record of them begins, the whole number is 724. Of their present residences and upon their occupations, I must be reluctantly silent, or only say, that of 72, we have lost all knowledge, and that 40 of our late or former number, are, or have been in the army or navy—that of these, seven will return no more by reason of death. Of Marriages, 42 females, and 19 male members, either present, late, or at some former time have entered the marriage state since the commencement of 1854—23 young men never members, have sought and found their brides in our Sabbath School, and led them to the altar,—and finally I mention the vase once filled with beautiful flowers, now changed to dried leaves, and smelling of death. Seventy-three late or former members have died since the beginning of 1850, 26 of them being abroad (including the Soldiers). One precious teacher Mrs. Cogswell and one dear pupil, Mary A. Andrews have died since this occasion was contemplated.

The whole number now enrolled is 338, of whom 184 are over 15 years of age —143 between 5 and 15—and 12 under 5,—91 belong to the Infant Department.

It is disagreeable to pass over the Sabbaths, the months and the *years* of our history in so much silence. Character has been developed sometimes with amazing rapidity. A small turn of the moral kaleidoscope, has often presented character in a new light entirely. The minds and hearts of children are being constantly developed, in some new and often unexpected form. Something of all this is known, but more is unknown, except as revealed by events, sometimes long years afterward. A boy has sometimes appeared to be attending closely to all that was said in Sabbath School, when it was subsequently found that he was meditating a robbery and really perpetrated it before sundown on the same day. Another would seem careless and would half break his teacher's heart, when there was afterwards some reason to think that under that unpropitious exterior there was a hopeful upspringing plant, and the boy was laying up treasure in heaven! One great *defect* in the working of the Sabbath School, is the want of power to collect the scintillations of thought struck out in the classes, and then bring them together, and let the rays commingle and the light be held up where all may see it. Who is to be the Prof. Morse of the Sunday School laying a telegraph wire from each class to the Superintendent's desk?

While upon this point of *bringing out character* in the Sunday School, I would love to recur to a few, perhaps forgotten incidents, and by many never known, for the reason that it may bear with advantage on the future. When in 1852 we were upon the character of Mary, last at the cross, and first at the Sepulchre, it seemed proper to ask for an imitation of that trait in *any cross bearing matter* relating *to the Sunday School*. We were then reviewing the Catechism publicly once a month. Some were occasionally absent on that day. I had had too much experience not to know, that there may be good cause for absence often repeated too. You may be too ill, in a world where pain is the side companion of man. One of our older members was absent in 1861 for which I could not at the time account, and it troubled me. It was afterwards known that the absence was for the purpose of ministering to the wants of a dying mother, and another, at another time, was about the bed of a dying daughter.

One of our early members, once sent me word giving the

reason of absence, I have forgotten the year, but never the message!

But let me repeat the rule to-day, laid down twelve years ago, that when God puts no sorrow in your path, beware how you put any obstacle to duty there.

It is no part of the female character to be too timid for duty; but there may be such a *misapprehension of it*, as admits of deserting our appropriate place. That person has never yet walked worthily through this world, who has had no painful duty to do. I once desired a young lady to read a piece upon the stage at one of our fourth of July celebrations. It raised a great conflict in her mind between her native modesty and her sense of duty. "*I don't see how I can,*" was her answer, "but if you wish me to, I will," smiling, "if it half kills me." And another of a great heart but waning life, and whose feet have brought her here with difficulty enough for years, was never known to draw back from duty. One of those "suns has set, O rise some other such." You know, dear friends, that classes have sometimes come and staid and gone away, when none could be found to act as teacher. *May that blot never stain the yet unwritten page of the opening fifty years.*

And now let me say, that having been upon a voyage of fifty years, we come to anchor for one hour in port. Owners, underwriters and friends, we bid you a hearty welcome on board our little *Barque*. You will demand to know what we have done and left undone. On our part, we ask your further orders, and take a new departure for the voyage this day.

What account, fellow teachers, have we to give of ourselves?

> What have we learnt, where'er we've been?
> From all we've heard, from all we've seen?
> What know we more that's worth the knowing?
> What have we done, that's worth the doing?
> What have we sought, that we should shun?
> What duty have we left undone;
> Or into what new follies run?

Smooth as the sea of the Sabbath School seems to be, must we not say it is as *deceitful* as *any other sea*. And that it abounds with dangers, to which we must not be blind. Oh may this christian mariner (Mr. Bullard) continue to hang out the flag, or float the buoy over the quicksands and the rocks, as he has so long been doing.

Is it not one of our great errors, that *we are too often satisfied with the apparent amount of* Bible knowledge, *while the unbroken power of sin remains in the heart?* We have heard of the blind man, who every day walked around the walls of Stirling Castle, with the door-keys in his hand, polished by the friction of many years. This turnkey would recite to those he met, any passage of Scripture whatever, started by *them*, without the error of a word. When I read *so much* of his story as this, I said, Oh that we were all blind like him! But ah! the word had *no place in his heart.* His evenings were spent in sin and shame! His heart was as hard as the rock upon which Stirling Castle was built!

We hope we do not forget to urge these dear ones to look to God in prayer, in the day when their troubles come, as come they will. When the poet Cowper was crushed down in school by the fear of a large, bad boy, and whom he knew better by his Shoe Buckles than his face, he used to go to God for help as well as he could, saying, I will not be afraid of what man can do unto me! "No prayer," said Rev. Mr. Laurie at the Sabbath School convention in Newburyport, "No prayer is inefficacious"

We have endeavored to encourage *Christian Benevolence!*

It may be said that when you have taught a child to give bread to the hungry, and water to the thirsty, you have made him Benevolent. But can he not go farther? Cannot the child understand that he should look farther? It *costs* something to prove to the widow of Scindiah the folly of *Suttee*! And can the child not understand what burning one's self to death means? Does any one believe that Sheik Tahar would ever have heard of, and embraced the Christian Religion, had not the contribution boxes been carried round in New England? And shall not the Sabbath School throw its mite into them? Does any one believe that Capt. Augustine Heard of Ipswich, commander of the brig *Caravan* of Salem in 1812, with all his benevolence, would ever have taken Harriet Newell, her husband, and the early missionaries, on board his vessel on their missionary voyage to India, had not the ladies of the Tabernacle and other Societies in Salem have thrown their gold necklaces into the contribution box. Sabbath Schools must make it up now, for *then*, they had not begun to be.

The sum of $1015 saved by our Sabbath School and brought together by little hands during the past fifteen years, we trust has wiped away some tears, but the best thing about it, is, that the *habit of saving and giving away* will be like a river rolling onward to the sea, and sometimes one which may overflow all its banks. Old habits, *especially* those of the *waster* and the *spendthrift*, *unless uprooted*, will prove, as Horace Mann said, an *Engine of forty Satan power*, for overthrowing *good* and establishing *evil*. They must be counteracted by antagonistic forces or all is lost. Old habits are the masked batteries of modern warfare, with this peculiarity, that with them we shall destroy not the *enemy* but *ourselves*.

We have said, we think our little gifts, administered by Missionary hands, have wiped away some tears. It is in a moral point of view, however, that they must be chiefly viewed. Let the Westminster Review continue to say if it will, that the so called christianity of this day is more troubled about the barbarians of *Borie Boda Gha*, than it is at the sight of a family pining in want at the next door; let it say so if it will, nay let the scorner delight in his scorning everywhere, but lay us a telegraphic wire from each of the *many* hearts that have been the recipients of our tiny gifts, and though we could not read the language of either Palestine or Ceylon, of either Madura or Koordistan, yet the sounds and sights of human woe can be understood any where, and we shall not ask the Westminster Review whether we may be satisfied. We may not even know the names of half the Micronesian Islands, but we helped to sail the Morning Star among them, and in an important sense, those islands are our islands. We have sent a hundred volumes to a destitute Sabbath School six miles from Marietta, and another Library to Moss Run, both in Ohio ; — a library to Bliven's Mills in Northern Illinois, a set of Pulpit furniture for the meeting-house at Isle au Haute, with a full supply of Catechisms for the Sabbath School at that lone island, a $25 Library to Illinois, an equal one where the books were read on the Mountains of Persia, and around the grave of Henry Martyn, a $20 Library for Seamen, a $20 Library to Illinois, $17 to Madame Feller's Mission in Canada, a Library to Bloomington, where the Mormon Stakes were up. We have made eighteen of our teachers members of the Massachusetts Sabbath School Society by the payment of ten dollars each, the whole amount having been expended by that Society. A Library has been sent to our Sooty cousins on the Coast of Africa. A token of sympathy of $17 to the founder of the Sabbath School then ill with a broken limb.

We have put $90 into the hands of the Sabbath School Union thus constituting three members of the school, members of that Society, the whole amount being expended by that Society in carrying on their operations.

And while allusion has been made to some things done or attempted by the school abroad, it may not be improper to refer to some of its operations at home. It was in 1842, that we contemplated procuring a Bible for the then new Pulpit. It was our custom in those years to decide *in advance* upon the number of Sabbaths we would contribute to a given object, and not to exceed that time in any case. But we had set the time too short for the Bible and it was laid here by other hands.

The Church Clock, however, in the same year was the gift of the Sabbath School, at the cost of $40—as well as $50 worth of Organ pipes in 1854.

These two sums are included in the $1015 contributed during the last fifteen years, but the avails of the two donation visits to a house of sickness (where the fig tree did not blossom) amounting in all to somewhat more than $100, was not so included, neither was the gift next to be mentioned.

Three little girls once taken up in a remote part of the town to ride a little way, though not then members of the Sabbath School yet because they said they were going to be, did more to give us courage than their little hearts could well conceive. This was *incidental*; but in what suitable words shall I, or can I, acknowledge the *intended* expression of gushing good will, with which the School *surprised* me on the second Sabbath of June 1857, when they put in my unworthy hands a rich collection of books, accompanied by a beautiful donation speech uttered by Susan E. Andrews, but written as I had afterwards reason to believe by the lamented wife of our kind Pastor!

If ever, during the labors of the last seven years, I have felt a moments weariness in this glorious work I have only to look at those Books. One of them alone contains the Biography of 2300 distinguished men and women of our own country, and there are few of them all whose example is not enough "to hang sorrow, and drive away care!" Then open Kitto's Cyclopedia of the Bible, of near 2000 pages more, written by forty independent minds, all men of great Bible Knowledge, and all Baptized with the Holy Ghost. And again, if for variety, I wish to take a voyage among the eternal snows of an Arctic Winter, I have but to look into Doctor Kane's great Books of Travels, all which books, dear friends, your love has made my own.

TOPICS.

As we have made so sparing a use of the Question book,

having had but *one* for thirty-two years excepting the Catechism monthly, I feel that it may be proper to refer more particularly to the *topics* studied than would be othewise necessary. Without giving at this time more than a brief specimen, it may be mentioned, that we endeavor, both in the classes and at the General Exercise to enforce and explain the lesson, both by precept, and by anecdote. The *Commandments* have received a large share of attention.

Perhaps violations of the 8th Commandment are *in the country*, as common as any, especially in the long fruit season. It seems a harsh doctrine, but we feel compelled to say that the seeds of dishonesty are sown in all our hearts. We first *cost*. Here we teachers must begin to fight ourselves, and arm the children to fight in this dreadful, though unbloody field. The Rev. Mr. Hildreth once told us, when illustrating the *inveteracy* of this sin, that when a confirmed thief was executed in England, he was by some mistake taken from the gallows before life was quite extinct, and removed to the dissecting room of the anatomist. When the surgeons afterwards entered, they found the thief *alive and* actively searching the room for something to steal," thus showing the ruling passion not only strong in death, but after death. No change had been effected in his character by what was supposed to be a change of worlds.

The Sixth Commandment opens the question relating to Capital punishment. How important to meet the terrible fallacies of our day on this subject! How much is yet to be done to get up a correct public sentiment. William Goode the vagrant or drunkard may be sent to the house of Correction and nobody complains, but William Goode *the murderer* had thousands of sympathizing friends.

A father gives his son a severe whipping for dulling his axe or plane-iron, and nobody cares, but Daniel A. Reardon may murder his wife and twin babes, and after a few months of imprisonment, the flickering, uncertain and impulsive public will run over the whole Commonwealth with petitions for his pardon.

And when we recollect the names of the two distinguished men, who have recently knocked at the Council Chamber door, demanding a murderer's pardon, and especially when the Chief Magistrate in 1862, publicly deplored the presence of the Death penalty on the Statute Book, is it not a wonder that Edward Green is not walking in the streets of Malden to-day; or perhaps doing up his unfinished business at the bank!

How glorious an institution is the Sabbath School inasmuch as it affords the lay element an opportunity to step forth for the defence of the institutions of our holy religion. I find a record of the fact that on one bright clear Sabbath day in July, in our own town, a wagon load of hay was unloaded in sight of the children, and all others on their way to or from the House of God. How important to hold up the fourth Commandment before the child's mind. And how I love to contemplate a Statesman or Politician planting his foot for the defence of the Sabbath! I have just now in mind the memorable fact that in the year 1844, when many religious institutions were in danger, and some for a time seemed laid waste, and when our own Legislature was gravely petitioned to pass a Law *withdrawing all protection from public worship on the Sabbath*, the chairman of the Judiciary Committee (Mr. Saltonstall) told the petitioners to take their miserable paper away!

In selecting topics according to taste or inclination it would be almost *natural* to study the case of Annanias and Sapphira struck dead with a lie upon their tongue. Of Nadab and Abihu who died for offering strange fire, and the men of Bethshemesh who died on the spot for looking into the ark. But all this while we find it important to guard all minds against the idea that this world is the place of retribution, that all men here receive the due reward of their deeds.

Not every blasphemer is a Morton South, after whose oaths his tongue became paralyzed, and his mind becomes idiotic.

The book of God's providence is to be studied as well as His Word, and the Sabbath School teacher should not fail to draw lessons from passing events and also learn to draw conclusions cautiously.

A bold infidel in Ohio built a house in 1847, and all the glass of that house was set on the Sabbath by his own impious hand. He wanted, he said, to live long enough to dedicate it with a ball, and so he did. "And there was a sound of revelry by night, and music arose with its voluptuous swell." But hardly had that music died away, when the Lord blasted the life and the house of that Atheist man, and the next morning's sun revealed the fact that every pane of that Sunday set glass was a broken pane, as well as the more terrible fact that the owner had danced his last dance.

But as if to keep us humble learners in the Saviour's School and to prevent our drawing hasty conclusions, God's Providence also teaches us that He sometimes waits and allows the potsherds of the earth to contend with their Maker.

Soon after reading of the scene in Ohio in the Home Missionary, while riding in Boston, I noticed a Bookstore with the gilded lettering, "Infidel Books at wholesale and retail." More triflers go down to death from that place, than danced upon the floors of the infidel's house on its first and last night, I apprehend, yet it pleased the Lord to destroy the less, and let the greater live!

Here is a field for the Sabbath School teacher showing that as a Great Sovereign, God may choose his own time and way for punishing the wicked as well as rewarding the good.

In 1863, we spent considerable time upon the subject of the *Sabbath* to which reference has already been made, and following that, a subject never before given out in the Sabbath School. MARRIAGE, we considered as the state to which with few exceptions, the human family have glanced an eye forward with more or less intensity, from a comparatively early age, indeed ever since the time when "Eve stood blushing in her fig-leaf suit." It is an institution older than the Sabbath itself. The leading idea however, enforced in the school related to the *example of the parties* at Cana in Gallilee, in *inviting Jesus and his disciples to the marriage*. There are those in the world who are rarely found among the people of God and more seldom still, among his ministers, and it is sometimes more agreeable to *them, to have the civil Magistrate solemnize the marriage*. (I have been called more than once to perform the ceremony). These are usually those who have no seat in God's house, and no Sabbath day to keep holy. I can almost understand how a *man of iron*, can come to prefer that no minister shall be present at either the bridal festivity or the funeral solemnity; but how the tender heart of a blushing bride could give her consent I cannot understand, and without that consent, you know, the door to married life is closed. Can any one doubt the propriety of giving this topic a place in the instructions of the Sabbath School? Can any one doubt that this is the place in which to plead that on the bridal day of life, whenever that day shall come, *both Jesus may be called and his ministers to the marriage*? Upon this topic the pulpit does not often speak, but the Sabbath School Teacher may. I have as yet seen no cause to regret that for once the mind of the School was turned *distinctly*, and not *incidentally* to this topic.

Neither have I ever yet regretted reading the story of Bertha and her Baptism by Dr. Nehemiah Adams, and remarking upon it with perfect freedom not because young ladies, while residing in our community are particularly liable to the dangers which Bertha encountered, when contemplating the marriage state. But many of our school have gone abroad and many more may go.

A teacher suggested a few weeks since that this occasion would afford a convenient opportunity for examining the question which still continues to agitate the public mind, whether the Sabbath School has not innocently and unconciously but *effectually* lessened family religious training. There is time for hardly a remark upon this point. The attention which I have been able to bestow upon it, however is gradually leading me to the conclusion that with many brilliant exceptions, family instruction was never so *universally* practiced even in New England as to leave no room for the Sabbath School. That the live oak timbers of multitudes of our youth were salted on the stocks and "seasoned with the incorruptible word that liveth and abideth forever," the whole New England character abundantly proves. But that even family religion might not *fall into decay* can hardly be doubted, since even in the household of holy Eli you find a neglected Hophni and Phinehas. In the absence of *direct proof*, something may be inferred from other sources. Our church records show, that in 1782, one year only, by an interesting coincidence, after Robert Raikes began his glorious Sabbath School career in England, the Rev. John Cleaveland, then our Pastor, and his church, saw the necessity of a similar measure here. The Church requested the Pastor, and Elders, "to consult and report a plan for districting the Families of the Parish for Catechising &c." It originated with Mr. Cleaveland of course. It was brought forward, on 17 June, in that year. The plan was to be reported August 28, but "the day was rainy, and but few present." On the first of September, same year however, the plan for *districting the parish for Catechising* &c., was read and discussed and unanimously adopted. I now stop to ask, why was all this necessary, *if family religion* was in that healthy condition that the modern objection to Sabbath Schools implies? Why was it necessary that pastor Cleaveland should come down from his study to catechise the children of the parish on a week day, walking through old Chebacco with the Bible in one hand, and Catechism in the other, leaving him time to write his sermons upon *two little leaves only*, of the size of a man's hand? Why I say was all this necessary, if the FAMILY was doing all it should have done, and this so soon after that Great Revival which brought one hundred into the church within six months.

That Deacons Seth Story, Senior and Junior, and Deacon Zachery Story, brother of the latter, used to catechise their children, there can be no doubt for *their descendants* like their *sepulchres* are with us unto this day. But that "Ginny John," catechised his, the very nick-name that has come down to us, seems to make doubtful unless the question was, why they drank so much of the liquor and left so little for him. And whether even Tinker J — - should have been much given to it among his, may be questionable, though we are pleasantly told, he used to *see dreams* and *hear visions*.

The importance of family training was felt and practised in very unequal degrees by different families, some over-doing as Cecil says was a common puritanic fault, and others under-doing, probably still more common. May it not have been a part of the true mission of the Sabbath School to equalize that family training. "William," said a father in this neighborhood, and who was led about the time the Sabbath School was started, to think he might have been a little remiss in duty, "William, who made all things?" If William had ever been told, he just then forgot, and instead of saying God, named the best man he knew of — - one of our Deacons!!

A *mother*, on the other hand, determined that the sin of *remissness*, should not be laid to her charge, and as usual began on Sabbath evening, "Mary, who was the first man?" Mary, who was perfectly tired of her repeated embassies to the garden of Eden, replied once for all by saying, "*Adam and Eve.*" Here there are examples of *excessive family* training in one house, and the utter destitution of it in another, both within a very short distance, and in one case the father, grand-father, and great grand-father of little William, were all Mr. Cleaveland's constant hearers, and two of them members of his church.

I am driven, therefore, to the conclusion, that the Sabbath School was a NECESSITY, both in England and America. In England, to stay the open desecration of the Sabbath, and in our country to hold up fainting parental hands where they were already up, and to help raise them where they were not. (Having referred to the founding of Sabbath Schools in England, I deem it but an act of justice to say that Rev. Mr. Stock acted with Raikes conjointly in the Sabbath School enterprise.)

The world seems full of facts, going to show the importance of bending the twig just as the tree *ought to be inclined*. O what an opportunity Sabbath School teachers have to *take up and finish* the *parents unfinished* or neglected work. It would be a monster of a mother who should fail to teach her lisping babe to say, "Now I lay me down to sleep," &c., and to the credit of all who intrust their children here, I may say, that of about two hundred present some years ago, there were not more than three, and I think but two, who did not know those four lines. But I equally well remember that not one of all that two hundred, could tell *when they learned to say them*. This beautiful prayer had been breathed into their ears by maternal lips, during the unconscious days of infancy. The great parental error was to stop too soon.

Whatever we may think of it, the minds of children are often made up even on the *doctrines* of the Bible, before we know it. When speaking of the Catechism, the infidel Parker said he trod the abominable thing under foot before he had seen his seventh birth day, and long before that time says this redoubtable, though baby theologian, "the doctrine of the Trinity, and that of a wrathful God, had gone the same road. Since then," says he, "I have had no desire for the narrow heaven, nor fears of the roomy hell of which men talk."

Not every mind, I admit, is capable of a course so awful; but it is always dangerous to neglect a child, while it is eminently hopeful to lead him in the way in which he should go.

But I must pass over much in order to refer to two or three years more, as briefly however as their importance will admit.

1849. The events, distinguishing this year, and which made it somewhat memorable, were that of committing and reciting the Assembly's Catechism at *four* or *fewer* lessons without the variation of a word or the least help from the teacher, together with the outpouring of God's Spirit, that so immediately and remarkably followed. Let it however here be distinctly said, and once for all, that it is to the *preaching of the gospel by the ministers of Christ*, that *we must ever look as God's great instrumentality for the conversion of souls; and any reliance on Sabbath School agency, or any other agency to the exclusion of preaching, God will never own, but He will in some way frown upon it, as he thundered upon the Egyptians with a very great thunder*. But He condescends to allow other means, as family instruction, and we may add, the Sabbath School. We began to entertain a strong desire to have the school thoroughly acquainted with that glorious formula of the doctrines of the gospel, the Catechism, and on appealing to the church for pecuniary aid, the church responded and authorised us to draw upon their treasury for such sums as should be needful for putting an English clasp Bible into the hands of all who should be entitled to it. On the third Sabbath in September a specimen Bible was held up before the School, and the *conditions* of receiving it were stated. Some said the church never need fear that they should have many Bibles to pay for on such conditions; but the soul of the school was fired; and on the second Sabbath in October, it was ascertained that sixty-five had commenced repeating the Catechism for the grand reward of the grandest effort ever put forth in the town. The *conditions were indeed stringent*. It was accomplished with many tears on the part of the learners. It also cost the teachers tears, to say, at the end of twenty-seven answers, "there was an error or two, but I must not tell you where. Go over the whole again." But with some exceptions, all who began, succeeded. The minister and the church were gratified. Parents smiled. The children smiled. But our crowning joy was, we thought the Lord from heaven smiled.

On the second Sabbath in December, the record of the Sabbath School states that twenty had finished the Catechism and were entitled to the Bible. That Bible, with the receiver's name engraved upon the clasp, was delivered *publicly*, with much thanksgiving to Almighty God, and many prayers for His blessing to follow. Those thanksgivings, we think, were accepted, and those prayers heard, and that blessing followed. On the first Sabbath in December, a memorandum on our records says, much interest in religion has appeared in the Sabbath School within a week. Four in one class, are entertaining hope. Between twenty and thirty met last evening in two different places for prayers, seeking the Lord. Indeed, the appearance of the school was so changed, so solemn, that we could not help exclaiming, "this is the Lord, we have waited for him, we will be glad and rejoice in his salvation." One extract more from the same memorandum says, "It was mentioned two or three Sabbaths ago, that a member of the school had hopefully passed from death unto life. Last Sabbath *another*, whose sins were many, hopes they are now forgiven, and next day another tongue broke out in unknown strains and sung surprising grace. Since that time many hearts have yielded the controversy with God. Some families have kept such a thanksgiving as they had never kept before. The kingdom of heaven seemed to suffer violence, and the violent seemed to take it by force.

On the third Sabbath in December, being but two and a half months from the time when the offer was made, forty-two Bibles had been delivered. The whole number to the present time is one hundred and seventy-eight.

We have sometimes called 1849, our happy year. *All,* certainly, were not so, *few,* indeed, were like it. The year 1855 contrasted strongly. Our numbers diminished that year, while neighboring schools increased. The attractions about town were too much for the Sabbath School. The river and the roads seemed scarred with sin. One boy, who left us, said he had got all the good there was to be had, *he* thought. Another said he had as lief go to hell as to the Sabbath School, and a third when asked by his teacher if he thought he could endure the judgment of the great day, boldly answered, yes! We know Dr. L. Beecher's rule, that such boys should never be allowed to *leave,* but should be publicly expelled. But we were afraid. Our tears became our sorrowful meat. The cloud at length however gradually lifted. These distinguished Boston friends had more to do with lifting that cloud than they have ever yet known of. Through their agency, Massachusetts and New York shook hands together that year in the Crystal Palace, and the recollection of what we there heard and saw, chased all our tears and our fears away together.

INFANT DEPARTMENT.

Our infant department was formed and organized as a branch of the main school, on the first Sabbath of May 1859. It consisted at that time of thirty-two members, Mrs. Caleb Cogswell, teacher, assisted for a time by Miss Mary S. Spofford. Mrs. Cogswell continued to conduct the department with excellent success until she left for a year's residence in Minnesota.

It was determined that this department should *begin at the beginning;* that the first question should be, "Who was the first *man;* and the second, who was the first *woman?* and to follow in the train of the book, which gives us these facts. Because, *that same first man,* by his Fall, lost communion with God, and came under his wrath and curse; and as by that one man, sin entered into the world, and death by sin, the children could begin to understand why so many little tombstones were decking the burial ground in the spring of that year; why some thirty weeping fathers had just then built their children's tombs. It was all because of *the fall of man*, that he and all his long posterity must die.

The late lamented Mrs. Bacon commenced teaching in the Infant Department, on the 17th of June 1860, Miss M. S. Spofford having found her health insufficient. The number had now increased to forty-eight. Mrs. Bacon conducted the department as her predecessor had done, with great success. Her manner of teaching, said a writer in the religious Papers, "was, *like herself*, affectionate and persuasive in the highest degree." Her labors ended only with her life. Blessed are the dead who die in the Lord, that they may rest from their labors, and their works do follow them. She died on the 31st of January, 1863.

From this time, 31st of January, 1863 Miss Maria W. Crowell heard the class as frequently as she was able, until the first Sabbath in July, when her waning health forbade her meeting with them any longer. She died on the fourteenth of November, having often spoken of the children with the deepest affection and many prayers. After the teacher's chair was vacated by Miss Crowell, it became occupied by the present incumbent, and now numbers ninety-one members, a great advance upon anything before.

It is, I presume, within our recollection that extensive blessings attended the preaching of the word and other means of grace in 1858. Our teachers felt it then, as in former years, only more so, to be their sweet and solemn duty to point to heaven and lead the way; to talk much of Christ and Him crucified; to pour forth their thoughts of that wondrous One; His life; His death; His everlasting presence, and His power to save.

With curiously *critical* teaching we felt that we had but little to do. The Boston Review tells us that the word Uzzen Sherah occurs but once in the Bible, but that important matters were connected with it. But we thought the salvation of the soul should transcend all other considerations. This was in that remarkable year, when the most extensive revivals of religion, ever known in our country or in Europe, were in progress; and it was now that the *third* outpouring of God's Spirit was experienced in our Sabbath School. Thirty-one, in the judgment of charity, passed from death unto life, and on the first Sabbath in July following, twenty-seven of them publicly professed their faith in Christ. Some others have followed since. We could but say as on a similar occasion in 1849: This too is the Lord: we have again waited for Him, and He has again come to bless us. O, that we could add, *every one of us*, in turning us away from our iniquities.

In bringing these somewhat disconnected thoughts to a close, I cannot allow myself to forget the obligations that our church and the rising generation are under: 1st, to the late Robert Crowell D.D., who founded this Sabbath School, and held it up so long by its infant hand. 2d, To our present pastor whose wakeful eye is upon the school with the same anxious assiduity, and whose presence is always sunshine in the school. 3d, To its first Superintendent for twelve to fifteen years, and who not long after collected the *first of our eight adult classes;* who has never failed of meeting that class on any but *sick* days, and those but few indeed, and who now in vigorous age, still stands up before some twenty adult members every Sabbath day "for to read" and expound; and 4th, to the long line of teachers for fifty years, both the living and the dead.

When I have been sometimes looking at the *town schools*, I have said to myself, how much good a teacher does that he is never paid for! for the interest taken! for the plans laid in the wakeful hours of night, all centering in the school room! midnight reviews of yesterday's work, or to-morrow's designs! But how insignificant all this becomes, when laid alongside of the debt which the rising generation owe to faithful teachers in the Sabbath Schools. I am free to own, that I have often received more pain than pleasure, at some State or other large Convention, when the speakers have been laying heavy burdens upon teachers' shoulders, as I thought already deeply loaded, almost requiring them, if I may change the figure, not merely to "roll away the stone," but to bring the sleeping Lazarus forth! If by the use of that bad word *unpaid*, or *non-paid*, I labor in the Sabbath School, I have raised the thought in any mind that teachers should be paid, let me say, the Sabbath School system will no more bear the touch of selfishness or *pay*, than, as Mary Lyon said, the Mt. Holyoke Female Seminary would, where it is known that every Trustee or Committee man *who took pay for service*, had but one short step from the quarter-deck over the ship's side. Sabbath School labor will not bear pay, I refer of course to labor in the school room.

If the American Churches owe that debt of gratitude to the 500,000 Sabbath School teachers which all great and good men say they do, then dear fellow teachers of this our Essex branch, a proportionate share is due to *you*. Your instructions have fallen upon seven hundred or a thousand minds. Your hands, I speak collectively of all the past as well as the present laborers in the field, have done what they could to fill these minds with God's word. And as the skill of the operator in our city churches, by one stroke of his art, lights a hundred lamps in an instant, so, says Dr. Nehemiah Adams, *regeneration* will convert the knowledge of the Sabbath School child, at once into a source of pleasure unspeakable.

In allusion then to the Marriage at Cana, I would use the words of the Great Guest, and say, "Fill ye then the water pots with water, *up to the brim*." Christ is near by, and can change that water all into wine in a moment.

Travellers tell us, that beautiful rivers, golden rivers, sometimes disappear under a burning sky, and seem lost in the sands, but you are sure to find them again bursting out in a more congenial clime, and thence rolling onward to the sea. So mental philosophers tell us, "the mind *never forgets*. The delicate tracery of early impressions may be lost a while under the sterner stamps of maturer years, but it is all there." Therefore, disheartened TEACHERS, SUPERINTENDENTS once of us, but now in more extensive fields of labor, dear Pastor of our own church, Life long laborers present, whose Sabbath School is the Commonwealth, Ministers, and men of God who gladden us with your presence to-day, "THEREFORE, I say, let us not be weary in well doing, for in due season ye shall reap if ye faint not."

Appendix to the Historical Discourse.

A

May 28, 1679. In ans. to the petition of the inhabitants of Chebacho, Wm. Cogswell, Sen., Robt. Crosse, Sen., William Story, &c., upon a full hearing of the Chebacho case, this Court judge the peticoners of Chebacho have offended the councel, in going expressly contrary to their advise, in erecting a meeting house, which they ought there imediately to acknowledge, & humble themselves for; as also, wherein they have justly offended the officers & church of Ipswich, wee order them seriously to apply themselves to the church for reconciliation; which being done, doe grant them liberty to procure a minister, to be helpfull to them in the worke of the ministry, provided he be pious, able, & orthodox, as the law directs, with the advise of the following committee, i. e., Joseph Dudley, Esq., Major Richard Waldron, Mr. Anthony Stoddard, Mr. Henry Bartholmew & Leift. Wm. Johnson, who are appointed to be a comittee for that affaire, & are desired to meete on the place at the peticoners charge & request, & to heare theire allegations, & the allegations of some deputed by the towne of Ipswich, referring to the accomodations of others of their inhabitants, & fynally to determine the place of erecting a meeting house that may be most acomodable for them; & all cases depending in Courts referring to this matter doe cease, & the Chebacho men are to pay tenn pounds for this Courts costs. As an addition or explanation of the order to Chebacho men, it is hereby ord-red, that such of them as are delinquents, in errecting a meeting house there contrary to the advise & prohibition of the council, & are sumoned to Salem Court to ans. their sayd contempt, doe there make their acknowledgments in these words, viz., that they are convinced that they have offended in so doing, for which they are sorry, & pray it may be forgiven them, & so to be dismissed with out any further trouble, charge, or attendance in that respect, or further attendance on the council for that their offence.

The Report of the Committee thus appointed, is as follows:

Ipswich, Jebacco, July 23, 1679.

The persons vnder written being a comittee of the honnorble General Court, as by their order, dated May 28, 1679, for the setlement of the buisnes of Jebacco, touching the place of publick worship amoungst them, & the setlement of a minister in that part of the towne for their acomodation in the worship of God & proppogation of religion amongst them, as in say'd order is particcularly recited, —

The say'd persons mette vpon the place, die supradicto, & there found present the peticoners & other inhabitants of say'd Jebacco, as also others that were deputed by the toune of Ipswich to offer something refferring to the acomodation of others of their inhabitants, & vpon a full hearing & serious consideration of what was offered & pleaded by both parties, doe find the p'sons, peticon's & others, ye inhabitants there, haue attended the order of the honnorable Gennerall Court, in humbly acknowledging their fault, in going contrary to the advice of the honnorable council, & in giving sattisfaction to the offended church of Ipswich, which, was allowed & attested by some of the reuerend elders, & other persons of credit members of the say'd church, & therefor doe conclude, —

(1st.) Refferring to the place of the meeting house, that though a remoove of the house from the place at present designed by said Jebacho inhabitants, farther towards the toune of Ipswich, might acomodate some more of the inhabitants, & farmers of say'd toune, yet, perceiving that the number offering themselues are competent for such a setlement, & those at the head & on the other side of say'd river of Jebacho will be much disadvantaged thereby, who were the first agreived & petitioning partye, that therefore the place where the house now standeth be & is heereby allowed by us, & that they haue liberty to proceede to the finishing of the say'd meeting house for their comfort & setlement.

(2dly.) Refferring to the setlement of a pious, able, & orthodoxe minister amongst them for the due mannagement of the worship of God, wee find that the persons, inhabitants of Jebacho, who are like to be a joint society in this setlement, should seriously consider with themselues, with invocation of God's name, of some meete person, able, learned & pious, that may be fitt to mannage the publick worshipp of God amongst them, some time betweene this & Tuesday, the day before the session of the Gennerall Court, in October next, vnto which time the comittee doe adjorne themselues there, to meet in Boston, there to give their approbation vnto such person for the minister to setle amongst them, earnestly entreating & advising them in the meanetime to lay aside all animosity, & to take such advice as may be beneficiall for their future setlement & good accord.

May 22th, 1680. The comittee aboue written mett accordingly, & the inhabitants of said Chebacho presented Mr. John Wise as a person vpon whom they have vnanimously agreed vpon for their minister, who is acceptable to us.

B.

LIST OF BOOKS OWNED BY THEOPHILUS PICKERING.

List of some of the books owned by the Reverend Theophilus Pickering still preserved and bearing his name and the date within: furnished by Miss Mary O. Pickering of Salem, who also communicated the facts of Mr. Pickering's family and of his life prior to his settlement in Chebacco, which are mentioned in the Discourse.

'T. P. 1719.' Compendium Theologiae Christianae. Authore Johanne Wollebio ss. Th. D. & in Acad. Basil Profess. Ord. Amstelodami cIɔ Iɔ xxxxii.

'T. P. 1716.' Book of Common Prayer 12mo. London, 1713.

'T. P. 1716.' Physico-Theology or Demonstration of the Being and Attributes of God from his Works of Creation by W. Derham, Rector of Upminster in Essex and F. R. S. London, 1716.

'T. P. 1718.' Astro-Theology, or a Demonstration of the Being and Attributes of God, from a survey of the Heavens, by W. Derham &c., London 1715.

'T. P. 1718.' The Whole Duty of Man &c.,—with Private Devotions—, London 1716.

'T. P. 1719.' Brerewood's Survey of the Languages in the World, and of the various sorts of religion thereon — 12mo. 1614.

'T. P. 1721 2.' Psalterium Americanum, by Cotton Mather, Boston, 1718.

'T. P. 1724.' The Jesuits Morals by a Doctor of the Colledge of Sorbon in Paris - translated from the French: folio, London 1670.

'T. P. 1724.' Hooker's Ecclesiastical Polity - folio London, 1611.

'T. P. 1724.' Howel's History. An Institution of General History, from the beginning of the World to the Monarchy of Constantine the Great. By William Howel, M. A. Fellow of Magdalen College in Cambridge: folio, London, 1661.

'T. P. 1743.' Fuller's Holy and Prophane States: folio, 1648.

C.

CHURCH ARTICLES OF FAITH.

The Church Articles of Faith and Discipline of the newly-gathered Congregational Church of Christ at Chebacco in Ipswich.

Whereas we the subscribers have seen it our Duty to congregate & Embody ourselves into a Church State; & as we are of opinion: That a Lax admition into the Ministry, & a Lax admition into the Churches & want of Discipline are the Bane of Churches.—

We the subscribers, & each of us for himself, Do therefore oblige ourselves, & each of ourselves Respectively, by these Presents, to stand, to abide by, & be governed according unto, the following Articles of Faith and Church government, viz:

1st. That we will have such officers as Christ Jesus has appointed & ordained in his holy word, viz: a Pastor or Pastors, Ruling Elders & Deacons: see 1. Cor. 12, 28; 1. Tim. 3. 2-10; 1. 5. 17.

2d. That no Person shall be admitted to either of said offices, Unless they have scripture qualifications Evidently appearing to the satisfaction of the Church. Titus 1. 5-9; 1. Tim. 3. 8-13.

3d. That the Church shall have the Sole power of electing & appointing all the officers of the Church. Acts. 6, 3.

4th. That the officers so elected shall be ordained to their several offices by Imposition of Hands. Acts. 6, 6; 14, 23.

5th. That no Person shall be admitted as member of our Church, but such as shall give a particular account of a saving work of the spirit of God upon his or her soul, to the satisfaction of the Church; & upon satisfaction given to them, then the Person or Persons desiring to join with us shall be propounded, fourteen days at least before admition. And if no Reasonable matter of objection be made, then such persons may be admitted, as members of the Church & not otherwise. II. Chron. 23, 19; I. Cor. 11, 27, 28; I. John 1, 3; II. Cor. 13,5.

6th. That upon admition of any member or members into the Church, the covenant with these Articles shall be read to the Person or Persons to be admitted, in the Presence of the Church, & upon their approving & consenting thereunto, they shall then sign the same immediately. Neh. 9. 3; 10, 28, 29; Is. 46, 1–5.

7th. That we will not admit of any Person to minister to us in holy things, who shall refuse to submit to an Examination of the state of his soul by such a number of the Brethren as the Church from time to time shall think fit to appoint; & shall give to them a satisfactory account of a work of grace wro't upon his soul; who shall also sign these articles, before he shall be ordained to the Pastoral care of this Church. 1. Pet. 3. 15; Rev. 2. 2; 1. John 4. 1; Neh. 9, 38.

8th. That no adult Person shall be admitted to Baptism without giving to the Church sufficient evidence of a work of grace wro't on his or her soul, & that the infants of none but such, the Parents of whom, or one at least, shall be in full communion with the Church, shall be admitted to Baptism. Mark 16. 16; Acts 2, 38, 39, 45; 8, 37; 10, 47, 48; 1. Cor. 7, 14.

9th. That if any Member or Members shall walk inconsistently with the gospel, & their profession of Christ, they shall submit to such discipline as is agreeable to the word of God; & upon their continuing impenitent, & refusing to submit to such wholesome discipline as God's holy word enjoins, they shall be publickly excommunicated from our holy communion, until such time as they shall give credible manifestation of their repentance. 1. Cor. 5, 11; Titus 3. 10; Matt. 18. 15–17.

10th. That if any member or members of any other Church whatsoever (saving such churches as hold communion with us) not excepting against any denominations of Christians shall at any time desire to sit down with us at the Lord's table, they shall not be admitted unless they have been with the Pastor and one or more of the Elders, and given them sufficient satisfaction about a work of grace being wrought on his or her soul. 1. Peter 3. 15; 1. Cor. 11, 27, 28.

11th. That the Pastor or Pastors with the assistance of the Ruling Elders shall be, and hereby are obliged to visit every respective Person belonging to the Church at least twice in a year, and examine them in respect to their state, & growth in grace. 1. Pet. 5. 10; Heb. 13. 17.

12th. That whenever the Sacrament of the Lord's Supper shall be administered, after paying for the necessary provision & furniture of the same, the remaining part of the collection that shall then be made shall be wholly & solely applied for the relief of the church, & for no other use whatsoever. Rom. 12. 12; 1 Tim. 6. 18. 19.

13th. That neither Pastor nor Elders shall invite any Person to preach, until they are satisfyed that he has a work of grace wro't on his soul. 1 John 4. 3; Rev. 2. 2.

14th. We believe that all the gifts & graces that are bestowed on any of the members, are to be improved for the good of the whole, in order to which there ought to be such a gospel freedom, whereby the Church may know where every particular gift is, that it may be improved in its proper place, & to its right end, for the glory of God, & for the good of the Church. Acts 18. 24. 25; Rom. 12. 6 8.

15th. The confession of faith agreed upon by the Assembly of Divines at Westminster we fully agree to in every respect, as to the substance of the same.

16th. We would always have recourse to the Platform agreed upon by the Synod at Cambridge in New England, A D 1648; & for the fuller explanation of our own sentiments respecting Church discipline, &c. we will always be willing to be guided thereby, with the following exceptions & emendations, viz: *Chap*. 1. at the close of the *4th Section*. Respecting human determinations upon times & places of Divine worship, being accounted as if they were Divine, we except against. *Chap*. 4. *Section* 4: Respecting a constant practice in meeting together for Publick worship & a subjection & silent consent to the ordinances of Christ, being sufficient to constitute a church, we except against. *Chap*. 6. *Sec*. 5: We think Pastor & Teacher are not distinct officers, but both may reside in one Person. *Chap*. 7. *Sec*. 2: The power of the Eldership respecting spiritual rule, we hold doth reside in them; jointly & severally, & may be accordingly exercised.

Chap. 10. *Sec*. 6: Respecting the Direction of a Council being necessary in order for a Church to remove their Pastor, we do except against: *Sec*. 8: We judge the Elders ought to call the Church together when desired by any one member, & whenever the church is mett, the brethren have a right one by one, asking leave to declare their mind, without interruption or hindrance, and that the Elders have no power to adjourn or dissolve meetings without a vote of the Church: *Sec*. 13: Respecting the Elders having a negative voice, we except against, as not being founded upon the Scriptures. *Chap*. 13, *Sec*. 4. Respecting magistrates having a power to force people to contribute for the support of the gospel, we except against, being not intrusted with the support of the same; that the church have power to deal with all such as will not, if able, contribute to the support of the gospel, we hold, and also that by the Holy Scriptures, Gifts may be received but not forced from any without. *Chap*. 14. *Sec*. 7. Upon that respecting Baptised Infants being in a more hopeful way of attaining Regenerating grace than others, we say: They have no more power to attain it themselves than unbaptized ones. *Chap*. 14. *Sec*. 9. Respecting the lawfulness of a worthy member partaking with profane and scandalous persons, we except against. *Chap*. 15. *Sec*. 2. Respecting the Churches calling in the Council of other Churches, we approve of, with this addition, viz.: when the church proceed to call a council, it does not in the least prevent or hinder the third way of communion, if occasion require, after such council be dismissed. *Chap*. 17. *Sec*. 9. Respecting the magistrates having a coercive power, or right to punish a church that rends itself off from the Churches, being by them judged incorrigible and schismatick, we except against.

17th. We think it our duty, and hereby each one of us doth for himself, oblige ourselves to pay towards the support of the Gospel amongst us, according to our respective abilities. I Cor. 9. 7; I Tim. 5, 18; Gal. 6, 6.

18th. Lastly, that if notwithstanding our great care in the admition of a Pastor or Pastors, or other officers, any or either of them should deny or walk contrary to these Doctrines, and persist therein, then in such a case said Person, or Persons, shall no longer have any power or authority in the Church, but shall be, and hereby are, debarred therefrom, until manifest tokens of their Humiliation and Repentance. II John 7. 10; I Tim. 1, 17–20.

Witness our hands which we now put in the presence of the great God, and a council of these Churches, viz.: one from Boston, and the other from Plainfield, this 22d day of May, Anno Domini 1746.

JOSEPH PERKINS,   JAMES EVELETH,
SOLOMON GIDDINGS, JR.,   THOMAS CHOATE,
THOMAS CHOATE, JR.,   FRANCIS CHOATE,
LEMUEL GIDDINGS.   JACOB PERKINS, JR.

D.

THE PRINCIPLES AND FUNDAMENTALS OF MR. JOHN CLEAVELAND'S FAITH.

1. I believe that there is but one God, infinite, eternal and immutable in his Being, infinitely wise, just, holy, good, merciful, true and great; yea omnipotent, omniscient, omnipresent and omnivigilant, in his Divine Attributes and perfections; existing necessarily and independently, on whom depend all other existent Beings.

2. I believe that in this undivided Godhead, there is a mysterious Trinity of subsistences or persons — Father, Son and Holy Ghost — one in substance, co-equal, co-essential and co-eternal in power and glory. *This is a mystery, I believe, but can't comprehend.*

3. I believe that this great and glorious God created all things, both material and immaterial for the Declaration, Manifestation and Display of his own Glory.

4. I believe that when God made man in his own image and likeness, as he did, he endowed him with power to fulfill the conditions of the covenant of works that he was made under; that he was to have life upon his fulfilling said conditions; and that he was to act, not only for himself as a single person but for his whole Posterity as their public Head and Representative; so that they were to be sharers with him as he should succeed, either well or ill.

5. I believe that man being left to the freedom of his own will, by the instigation and seduction of Satan fell from that state of rectitude, holiness, Justice and innocence in which he was made, into a state of sin and misery, alienation and death, corporal, spiritual and eternal:

That by this fall he lost communion with God, having the powers and faculties of his soul entirely polluted, vitiated, and filled with enmity against a holy God, and all true holiness:

That hereby he with his whole posterity lost all power and will to do anything in the least pleasing to God, and had his mind so blinded as to call evil, good, and good, evil.

6. I believe that God from all eternity was self-moved, out of his sovereign good will and pleasure, to elect and predestinate a certain particular and determinate number of Adam's posterity to Eternal Life; and that God the Father entered into a compact and covenant of Redemption with the Son of his Love, to free them from a state of sin and misery and to bring them into a state of reconciliation, bliss, and everlasting Glory:

That in order that the Son of God should fulfill his engaged part in this Covenant, he took to himself, in a new relation by a hypostatical union, a soul and body of our human nature; and this Immanuel, being holy, harmless and undefiled, fully obeyed the Law actively, and entirely satisfied all its righteous demands, by his once offering up himself, a sacrifice to satisfy Divine Justice:

That hereby he consecrated a way into the Holy of Holies by his own blood, that whosoever will, may come and take of the water of life freely, gratis:

That hereby the way is opened for the descent of the Holy Ghost to work in us both to will and to do of his good pleasure.

7. I believe that those and only those that are elect according to the foreknowledge of God, are in due time effectually called out of darkness into marvelous light, by the supernatural operations of the Holy Spirit:

That they be hereby convinced of actual and original sin and transgression of the righteousness of God's holy law — the righteousness of God's sovereignty — and the necessity of a perfect and pure righteousness in order to stand before God in peace:

That they are convinced by Divine illuminations of the completeness and suitableness of Christ's righteousness for persons in just such circumstances as they are in:

That by the effectual power of the most high God, they are brought to obey the call of God, in embracing Jesus Christ as their Prophet, Priest and King, cordially acquiescing in and consenting to the way and terms of salvation through Christ.

8. I believe that they are justified freely for the sake alone of the imputed righteousness of Christ, received by faith without the deeds of the law in the least regard :

That this faith is the gift wrought by the power of God in the soul (being the first act of the *new creature*) ; and that Gospel repentance is concomitant with faith in *time*, and consequent upon it in the order of *nature* :

That the evidences of justification are ; 1. Faith that works by love ; 2. Sanctification in the Heart ; 3. The Spirit of God witnessing with our spirit that we are the children of God.

9. I believe that all justified persons are endowed with a spirit of adoption influencing them to cry *Abba Father—My Lord and my God* :

That this adoption exists by virtue of their union to Jesus Christ their Head and husband, elder brother and joint heir :

That their union to him is a mysterious divine union, being made one with him, yet so as he remains very God, and they very finite creatures as to the dignities of their persons or capacities or faculties.

10. I believe that santification does begin in the souls of believers when the act of justification is passed in their souls (or that justification and the beginning of santification are instantaneous,) and is carried on progressively and perseveringly till they are made complete in holiness by the same Spirit that effectually calls them :

That they never will be complete in holiness, while in these mortal tabernacles of our fleshly bodies.

11. I believe that true justifying faith is a living and not a dead faith, and is evidenced by good works (agreeably to the holy law of God, which I take to be the rule of the christian's life) flowing from a principle of life or Divine love :

That no works are pleasing to God before faith in Jesus Christ, from us rebels ; and consequently God will graciously hear no prayers with delight which are not put up to him in faith, notwithstanding the high obligation there is upon all rational creatures to pray continually to God, whether converted or unconverted.

12. I believe that Jesus Christ has an invisible church, his mystical body, made up of all the believers (or saints) in heaven and on earth.

13. I believe that Jesus Christ has a visible church here below, made up of those that in the judgement of charity do believe with the heart and confess with the tongue—who visibly covenant and agree to walk in all the ordinances and commands of Christ blameless :

That this church has power from Christ to choose such officers as he hath appointed to be in his church, viz. : Pastors, Ruling Elders and Deacons :

That they are to be ordained and appointed to their several offices by imposition of hands ; which power of ordination, Jesus Christ who is the true Head of his church has given to his churches as their privilege :

That every member of this church is under obligation to use the gift given him by Christ for the edifying of the body;

That such a church is to walk together in brotherly love, both officers and brethren, not seeking superiority and preeminence; remembering that there is but one Head, even Christ Jesus, who is God blessed forever;

That the members of such a church are to have a mutual watch over one another to stir up and exhort one another, to provoke to love and good works; and that in case God should condescend to refresh his saints with the Heavenly gales of his overflowing love, so as with a shout of triumph they should be constrained to breathe out acclamations of praise to the Lamb of God, the whole should rejoice with them.

14. I believe that there are but two sacraments to be observed in the Gospel church, viz.: Baptism and the Lord's Supper;

That Baptism is to be administered to none but visible believers and their infant seed, and is an external initiating seal of the covenant of Grace;

That the Lord's Supper belongs to all true believers in Christ that can act understandingly in the participation of it; and that it is designed as a means to refresh, comfort, establish, feed, nourish and confirm the saints of God in faith, love, humility and patience.

15. I believe that the record of God in the Old and New Testaments, is in itself a perfect Rule, and in the hands of the Holy Spirit, leads and guides us to heaven;

That it is life and spirit, marrow and fatness to the believing saint; that it contains great and precious promises in Christ for believers only, and awful and tremendous curses for all unbelievers, while such.

16. I believe in the resurrection of the just and the unjust, which will be at the final consummation of this world.

17. I believe that we must all stand before the Bar of God to be *tried* for an endless eternity.

18. I believe that the saints at this decisive day will be openly acquitted and absolved from all sin, guilt and bondage, and be made perfectly blessed and happy in the full enjoyment of God to a whole eternity.

19. I believe that Jesus Christ — the Lamb slain — will be the glorious judge of Quick and Dead.

20. And lastly, I believe that at this great and awful day of inquisition or judgement, the wicked unbelievers and all ungodly men will receive from Christ their awful and final sentence of eternal condemnation, and shall be committed into the state of exquisite torment for ever and ever.

E.
MR. CLEAVELAND'S PETITION TO THE COLLEGE FACULTY.

"To the Rev'd and Hon'd Rector and Tutors of Yale College in New Haven.

Rev'd and Hon'd: —

It hath been a very great concern and trouble to me, that my conduct in the late vacancy has been such as not to maintain interest in your favor, and still retain the great privileges that I have enjoyed for three years past under your learned, wise and faithful instruction and government. Nothing of an outward nature can equally affect me with that of being henceforward wholly secluded from the same.

Hon'd Fathers, suffer me to lie at your feet, and entreat your compassionate forgiveness to an offending child wherein I have trangressed.

Venerable Sirs: I entreat you, for your pastoral wisdom and clemency, to make in my case such kind allowance for the want of that penetration and solid judgment expected in riper heads — as tender parents are naturally disposed in respect of their weak children. But more especially I beg to be admitted in the humblest manner to suggest as a motive of your compassion to the ignorant — that I did not know it was a trangression of either the Laws of God, this Colony, or the College, for me as a member, and in covenant with a particular church, as is generally owned to be a church of Jesus Christ, to meet together with a major part of said church for social worship. And, therefore, do beg and entreat that my ignorance may be suffered to apologise. For in respect to that fact, which to riper heads may appear to be a real transgression, I can assure you, Venerable Sirs, that I have endeavored to keep and observe all the known laws, and customs of College unblamably. And I hope I shall for the future be enabled so to do, if I may be restored to a standing again in my class. Thus begging your compassion, I subscribe your humble servant and obedient pupil.

John Cleveland.

New Haven, Nov. 26, 1744."

The conclusion of the "Admonition" is as follows:

"Whereupon it is considered and adjudged by Rector and Tutors, that the said John and Ebenezer Cleaveland, in withdrawing and separating from the public worship of God, and attending upon the preaching of a lay exhorter as aforesaid, have acted contrary to the laws of the Colony, and of the College, and that the said Cleavelands shall be publicly admonished for their faults aforesaid, and if they shall continue to justify themselves, and refuse to make acknowledgment, they shall be expelled."

F.

EXTRACTS FROM MR. CLEAVELAND'S NARRATIVE OF THE REVIVAL OF 1763-64.

Inasmuch as it hath pleased God, who is rich in mercy, to visit us of late, in these parts, with the gracious influences of his blessed Spirit, in the conviction and hopeful conversion of many persons; more especially in Chebacco, which belongs to Ipswich, of the province of the Massachusetts Bay: And as we are to declare God's doings among the people, and to make mention that his name is exalted; I have some time had it in my heart, to give a short narrative of this work.

The Public have, some years since, been informed of the grounds and reasons of the people of my charge becoming a distinct worshipping assembly from the second church and parish in Ipswich.

I was ordained their pastor, Feb. 25, O. S. 1747, by a Council of Congregational churches. The church I stand related to as pastor, in point of church discipline and government, is strictly congregational according to Cambridge Platform; and in point of doctrine quite orthodox according to the New England, or Westminster Confession of Faith, or their catechisms. And in point of experimental religion, consists of such in general, before the late work, as profess to have met with a change of heart in the time of the more general reformation, which was in 1742, and thereabouts: And altho' God never left us without witness of his gracious presence with us under the administration of gospel ordinances, and there were some few instances of hopeful conversions in the time of the general declension of Christians, yet we must acknowledge with shame, that we rendered not again according to the benefits done to us, but greatly lost our first love.

Sometime in the month of October, this year 1763, the Rev. Mr. Francis Worcester came to preach to my people one Sabbath. He came early in the week and preached several lectures before the Sabbath and several after, and took his leave of us with a lecture to young people; and as their attention was roused by his other discourses, divers things in this took such fast hold on their consciences, that they could not shake them off.

A little while after, I exchanged with the Rev. Mr. Samuel Chandler, of Gloucester, and as he understood there was a number of persons under awakenings in my congregation, he adapted his discourses to their case, and his preaching that day was own'd of God for the begetting convictions in some, and for increasing them in others. They now frequented our religious conference meetings, and at these, I had an opportunity of discoursing to them more particularly about the great concerns of their souls; and once a week the young people assembled at the house of one of our deacons, besides the weekly conference, when I had an opportunity of discoursing to them familiarly of their soul concerns.

In the afternoon, Mr. Parsons preached a very suitable sermon; the meeting-house was as full of people as it could be; people came from the parishes all around us: There was a solemn silence thro' the whole assembly during the time of divine service, and a sacred awe on every countenance; never did I see an assembly more solemn before! It was near nine o'clock this evening, before the people could be prevailed with to leave the meeting-house. As the people were now inclined to assemble for religious exercise, and their attention was roused, I appointed another lecture to be on Friday this week; and from this time till the Spring business came on, we had two lectures in the meeting-house every week, on Tuesdays and Thursdays: The first was the most remarkable week I ever saw; and from that time to the Spring, our meeting-house was crowded as full as it could hold when we met, both on the Lord's days and week days.

Divers persons from other towns and parishes, were bro't under concern, viz.: from Ipswich-town and the Hamlet, Gloucester, Manchester, Beverly, Wenham, some from Topsfield, Rowley, Linebrook, Byfield, Newbury and Newburyport; and divers were hopefully converted.

Divers ministers came over to our help, and preached on our lecture days. And there was not a sermon preached, as I could learn, but what was attended with the blessing of God, either to bring on conviction of sin in some, or to bring comfort to others; that is, to bring some out of darkness into light, and to comfort and refresh such as had received light and comfort before.

As a considerable number of our young men, who were bro't under concern at the beginning of this work, remained under concern, exceedingly bowed down for divers weeks, we tho't it proper to turn our Tuesday lecture into a day of fasting and prayer for them, and for the pouring out of the Spirit upon all; and it was a remarkable day, some new instances of persons bro't under convictions, and several of these that had long been bowed down were made free, I trust, by the Son, so as to be free indeed.

Towards the last of February, divers persons having signified their desire to make a public profession of Christ, and to be admitted into the church in full standing, I gave notice that the Elders of this Church would meet at my house, such a day, to hear and take down in writing, the gracious experiences of such as had a mind to be admitted members of this church.

On the day appointed, such a number met as filled my house; I began to write a little after ten o'clock in the morning, and never rose from the table till about sun-setting; I took down some of the most material things, in the experience of twenty and two persons, from their verbal relation to the Elders. Now I had an opportunity to judge of the nature of the work, and was surprised to hear what great things God had done for many, who were very carnal and vain but a few months before! When I arose from the table I went into another room, where the people were chiefly gathered, and it was as full as it could hold, and I stood astonished! I never saw anything equal to it before; the room appeared full of God! Not a person to be seen but what was at prayer, either for themselves, or over some particular person or other in distress.

About a month after this, we took into the Church thirty and two persons more; and the whole number of those we admitted in the space of seven or eight months, was upwards of ninety, but above two-thirds of them were females. I have heard that the Rev. Mr. Parsons of Newburyport, admitted about that time, upwards of fifty; and the Rev. Mr. Jewett of Rowley, about thirty; and the Rev. Mr. Chandler of Gloucester, a considerable number, but I have not heard how many.

In the Fall of the year, and especially near that season of the year, that the work so remarkably began a twelve month before, there was not only a considerable revival of those who had received comfort; but several new instances of hopeful conversions, and divers bro't under convictions, who had been pretty secure, and the convictions of others revived. And the next day after the Anniversary Thanksgiving this year (1764) was kept by as congregation as a day of thanksgiving, for God's remarkably gracious visitation to us with his divine influences, the preceding year.

G.

PASSAGES FROM "CHEBACCO NARRATIVE RESCUED, &c."

Now view the separation at Chebacco, and see what they have done; and whether it deserves the name of a separation. Have they separated from the faith profess'd by these churches? No, they adhere close to it. Have they separated from the established rule of order, worship and discipline, of these churches? No, they have got nearer to them than ever; are more exact and careful if not more conscientious too, than is common. These things are indubitable. Well, what in the world is the matter? What have they done, that renders them scandalous? Where are those corrupt principles and wicked designs to be found, they are so often charged with in the answer. There is a good cry indeed, and not only the city but the whole country, according to some, must be hurried and huddled together to view this great sight; this new thing that has happened at Chebacco, and to express their resentments. Well, suppose they should assemble, what matter of wonder would they see? Why this they would see; that a number of christians that us'd to meet and worship God on the west-side of the road, now meet for that purpose on the east-side. They would find that instead of their sitting under the preaching and administration of their former pastor, now deceased, who they did not like, and under whose ministration they could not profit or be easy; they sit under the ministration of Mr. Cleaveland, whom they do like, and by whom they are better edified. They would further see, that instead of a lecture once a month, they have it once a week; and that instead of living without some of the officers the constitution requires, as formerly; they now have them. In short, they would find their doctrines sound and orthodox; their discipline strict, yet tender and moderate; their worship serious and devout, and their lives sober, humble and discreet. They would find them willing to pay all their behindments due to their deceased pastor; and that they have made proposals of reunion with the adhering part of the church and parish, and yet could not obtain so much as a conference for that purpose. It's true, they would also find that they had left without leave the society and communion of the pastor and church, who had used them so ill, as has been represented; and which, if it did not amount to a total subversion of the ends of the gospel, yet it was a great clog and hindrance to their edification. And with respect to the priviledges of the members under such difficulties, they were totally deprived and left without hope of it's ever being otherwise. And this is what they plead, for their separation from that pastor and that sett of members. And that's all they have to do. For, from the faith and fellowship, worship and discipline, communion and order of these churches, they have not separated. And what great cause of wonder would arise from all this? And in what respect would it deserve the frowns of the spectators? Is not here a mighty bustle about a very little matter? A great out-cry for no great cause? Yea worse, a threatening of censure on pretence of the breach of order, and of the constitution. When the case is quite otherwise; so far from a breach of the constitution and order of these churches, that it is rather a resumption and reavowment of it. As whatever they have varied from the constitution, in this act, may I think fitly be compared to a vessel carried out of her course or latitude by a side wind or cross current, which puts about, and stands seemingly back, to regain the same: Or to a traveller who has been led or forced out of his road, who treads back his wrong path in order to get right.

I answer and freely own, that in the first of those religious operations, some persons were too warm, and apt to censure others, and in some cases appeared more showey than was decent, as I apprehended. But then you must observe, that what they were so warm about, was the great things in religion; which methinks should in some measure plead their excuse. They adhered to, and earnestly contended for the faith, and other doctrines of the reformation, in maintenance of which the martyrs embraced the stake; and to which also our forefathers adhered. Nor did I ever perceive, who had opportunity of observing them, that the Antinomian errors got ground among them. A holy life and walk with God, their hearts were much set on; they apprehended with the apostle, that they ought not to fashion themselves according to the customs of this world; that the gospel prize was weighty, and required more wrestling and striving for, than most men were aware of. They had a quick and tender sense of divine things; they tasted that God was gracious; and that his word was sweet, and they loved it exceedingly, and the like. Hence they were hardly easy but when in religious exercises: And as every nature delights to promote its kind, they would frequently call on others, not only to be helpers of their faith and joy, but to share in it themselves: And when they met with neglect and cruel reproaches, as sometimes they did, they were too easily caught in the snare of impatience, and their own spirit perhaps being over-heated, as I believe is common in such cases, they sometimes spoke unadvisedly with their lips, in way of censure and reproach of others. And they that well knew the whole of the matter will, I am persuaded, say, they had too much provocation. They have been long since convinced of this error, and behave with the meekness becoming christians. However, great advantage was made of these things; they were multiply'd and aggravated then, as we find them now in the answer; and indeed, to such a degree did those calumnies proceed, and such a clamour was raised about this set of people, not only in that place, but elsewhere, as I think was more than proportionate to their failings, if not more than can well be reconciled with the spirit of christianity, or than was for the service of religion.

Let the pastor and church be never so much to blame in former times; yet at length they make up all, and do their duty; agree to have council; but then the aggrieved will not. No, their majority, fourteen out of twenty-six, refuse it. (Page 15.) And here at last you have found a resting place for the sole of your foot; a something, whereby to justify you, and bring you off, under all your former neglect, which otherwise you have own'd, would not be excusable; and now turn the whole blame on the aggrieved. Hence also, principally, you would make out your pretensions of falshood in the narrative, and justify all the calumny and reproach, with which you have loaded the authors. Hence, you would represent them as artful, plotting, deceitful; and in short, as vile a pack of knaves, as ever were. This you place as a castle within your tottering walls, and frequently fly to it when they tumble; as for want of foundation, and suitable materials they often do, even while you are endeavouring to build them up. This you sew as pillows under your arm-holes, and fix as bladders to support and keep you from sinking under the weight and justice of the cause, you are endeavouring to overset. You repeat, multiply, and magnify this thing; you use it negatively and postively; dress, new dress, and new shape it, and make it serve to purposes, more than one could well imagine. In short, it is the burden of your song, and almost become stale, and a by-word in your answer. It's plain you esteem it as your dernier resort, and as a city of refuge, on almost every occasion; and when you are failing, here you catch and here you hang; as every one that reads your answer, may see. But, alas for you, your fingers must be knock'd off this hold; your refuge will prove but a refuge of lies. This bladder must be pricked; these pillows, this prop, must be pluck'd away. This castle, from whence so many arrows dipt in gall, have been shot out against the aggrieved, their narrative, and their cause, must be demolished. And what will become of your confidence then? Must it not be as the spider's web, and as the giving up of the ghost?

It seems by you, that no preacher is more than a pretender, if he preaches with a little more warmth and vigour than is consistent with people's going to sleep under his sermon, tho' never so close, evangelical, sound and orthodox in his discourses. No, these must be contemned as pretenders, while not a cold, formal, or Arminian preacher, can be found in the country, to bear any part of your contempt and resentment.

"Stealing away the hearts of the injudicious." So you see, if any minister of this character wins a person to a good liking of his preaching, the minister must be a thief, and the man a fool. And just so it was in the apostles days; all men were fools, that they caught by this sort of guile, for they stole many a heart in this way; and a great disturbance it was then accounted, as well as now. However, I plead not for men's intruding themselves into other men's parishes; nor do I know that any great disturbance has been given to ministers of late by this means. However, if there is, I would suggest something that I am satisfied will remove it; namely, to treat the ministers and christians of the new-light character with a little more justice and candor, and not on account of some past disorder, that if left alone would soon die with age, go on to despise, disparage, and discourage them, as heretofore they have done; while nothing material can be objected to their soundness in christianity; and instead thereof turn their displeasure against the broachers and maintainers of such tenets as are subversive of the gospel. And this will secure the hearts and minds of their people; which otherwise are so injudicious they cannot be satisfied.

And I have as little doubt, but when the discovering and decisive day comes, to which your answer, with a strange security, I think, (considering what it is) appeals; when the question will not be, who has been most artful or powerful, or made most ado about order; tho' this last is good and a duty in its place and measure: But who has most strove to promote the spiritual kingdom of Christ in the world; who has most contended for the faith of Jesus, and for the edification and comfort of the saints, who has been most just, merciful and kind to his fellow-servant, and most laboured to loose the heavy burdens, and let the oppressed go free. Then, I say, I have no doubt but the cause of the aggrieved, and those who have appeared for them, will meet with a gracious acceptation from the Judge: Tho' they now sit pensive and silent, and somewhat low like the Myrtle Grove; not only on account of reproaches, but also and principally in regard of the withdraw of the Holy Spirit, which they may with reason, in part look upon as the effect of their own failings.

Truth and righteousness will never rot; no, cover them with what sort of filth you will, yet when that day comes, if not before, they will get uppermost, and go forth as brightness, and as a lamp that burneth.

H.
OFFICERS OF THE CHURCH

since the death of those who are mentioned in the latter part of the Historical Discourse, with the dates of their election and of their resignation or death.

DEACONS.

Caleb Cogswell,	1862.	Caleb S. Gage,	1873.
Leonard Burnham,	1873–1880.	Francis Goodhue,	1874.
David L. Haskell.	1880.		

CLERKS.

Caleb Cogswell,	1863–1875.	Rufus Choate,	1875.

TREASURERS.

Robert W. Burnham, 1874—d. August 13, 1876.
Mrs. Mary C. Osgood, 1876.

SUPERINTENDENTS OF THE SABBATH SCHOOL.

Caleb Cogswell,	1873–1878.	Rev. John L. Harris,	1878–1879.
George F. Mears, Esq.,	1879–1881.	David L. Haskell,	1881–1882.
George F. Mears, Esq.,	1883—d. March 6, 1883.		
David L. Haskell,	1883.		

www.ingramcontent.com/pod-product-compliance
Lightning Source LLC
Chambersburg PA
CBHW020827230426
43666CB00007B/1131